This book is dedic
beloved daught
January 28,

and travel. She swam with sharks in Australia, kissed dolphins in Mexico, cycled in France and dug up the roots of her mother's family in Italy. She had booked a trip with friends to France in March, 2018. She was planning on attending a cooking school later in Italy and on spending Christmas 2017 in CUBA!

The world was Lori's oyster and she a pearl in our World!

A Tribute To The People Of Cuba

We must also dedicate our story to the industrious Cuban peoples like Wilber, Rublio, Matilda and Juan the one armed baker, Mary Lou and her family that sheltered us and Vladimir, yes, Vladimir a holdover from the USSR days! Meet those and so many more that helped Pat & Cat along the highways and byways of Cuba. To all these and the other peoples of Cuba that live their lives daily with shortages of food and medical supplies due to their Government's stance on issues and our U.S. Government's illogical embargo! Cuba never waged war against the USA. Can this be because of Cuba's Communist Government? Remember Vietnam? Didn't we kill millions there and leave behind the blood stains of 58,000 young Americans in the soils of Vietnam? Since 1994 the U.S. embargo on trade with Vietnam was lifted and exports from Vietnam to the United States rose dramatically.

The question now remains, why do we continue to so severely penalize the Cuban people with embargo? Could it be the more than 1,000,000 Cuban refugees living and voting in Florida that continue to exert pressure on U.S. Politicians?

I

Cuba, the Forbidden Island

By Pat and Cat Patterson

Why Did They Cut Off His F***'n Hands?

There is no better way to feel a country, a culture or their politics than riding a bicycle through the midst of that country. This bike ride became more than just a bicycle trip. Our cycling adventures have allowed us insight into the lives and varying lifestyles of peoples around the world. *It changed our lives!*

Che Guevara went on a bicycle ride while in university. He was shocked by the abject poverty and the peoples terrible existences he witnessed in his home country Argentina, and in Bolivia. It changed his life!

Our three weeks in Cuba was an exploration of the Forbidden Island. It became a voyage seeking truth about the Revolution, the life of Che Guevara, and a lesson in Cuban history. While cycling through seventeen countries in Africa we wondered why there were so many posters and t-shirts bearing the image of Che Guevara so far afield from Cuba? Hated, feared and loathed by some, loved and a hero to so many others.

They killed him then cut off his hands. The USA, and our CIA, as well as the Green Berets had their finger-prints all over his execution.

We met travelers in Cuba from around the world, traveling freely yet we, citizens from the *land of the free* are forbidden to travel in Cuba? What set off to be a bicycle tour became a protest. We enjoyed the ride, hope you'll enjoy the read!

II

Cycling the Forbidden Island

Cuba, like the world, is not flat! Cycling up her spine, once we cleared the Sierra Maestra, we discovered plenty of little ups and downs on the road and with the weather. We found ourselves constantly in the remaining clouds of Hurricane Wilma and a dark cloud of money issues. The conversion from Mexican pesos to CUCs, or kooks, as the foreign currency is called locally, was costly. And, getting an understanding of how to pay in the Peoples Cubano pesos was a learning experience, too. Beyond these issues, thanks to friendly Cubanos, Pat & Cat enjoyed a wonderful bicycle ride during their three-week stay on The Forbidden Island.

We were limited to three weeks due to money problems. The exchange rate then was prohibitive and we had no chance to gather more funds. No ATMs, no credit cards. The resorts are clustered along the coast which meant fast rides down and slow pulls back up. We chose to invest our time with Cubanos rather than tourists.

If you're from the USA and haven't traveled to South or Central America you will probably return thinking the Cubans are living in poverty. However you don't see abject poverty like we've seen while cycling through Africa and the Americas. We didn't see any homeless or unfortunates living on the streets or in shacks. We DID learn that unlike all other nations in the Americas except perhaps Canada, Cubanos all have access to health and dental care and almost unlimited education. Also, all are given dietary sustenance above levels we had witnessed in many places. Life in Cuba, during our voyage, appeared to be above the poverty line. We saw few police, and no military or homeless people.

Chapter 1: Embargo, Sneaking Into Cuba, History, and a YAK
Why Did We Decide to Cycle Cuba?
*Was It Because They Cut Off His F***'n Hands?*

The United States of America and our CIA, so feared and loathed this man that they left their fingerprints all over his murder!

While cycling on our *Around the World Bicycle Odyssey* we saw Che in many places. It wasn't until our ride through seventeen countries in Africa that we developed a curiosity about him. Of course we'd heard of Che, who hadn't? Yet we began to marvel at his far reaching impact. Why did we see so many young men there wearing Che's iconic image on their t-shirts? Why had his likeness lived on globally for more than forty years since his death? Why was he better known in Africa and South America than Fidel Castro? What roads led Che from the soft life of a doctor in Argentina to the life of a Cuban Revolutionary and death, in just eleven years?

We have always been proud to be Americans. However, we haven't always been proud *of* America. All too often we see expressions of *nationalism* among our fellow countrymen who feel they are *patriotic*. Hearing Americans say, "We are the best, have the best, invented all the best," gives us great concern. Most of those chanting "USA, USA, USA" have never been and often never will travel outside the USA.

Remember the angry crowds throughout South America shouting and carrying signs, "YANKEE GO HOME"? This was commonplace during my youth. I was raised in a diehard John

Birch Society, Republican family. We couldn't understand why they wouldn't want us to fight for their freedom and democracy? Travel has brought us to the realization that most people of the world like us as individuals but sometimes dislike the things our government promotes or forces upon them.

Back then most of Central and South America was under the thumb of the CIA. More than a spy organization, the CIA at that time was tasked with controlling other governments. A lot of elected leaders in those countries were deposed because their philosophies were socialistic. They were usually replaced by right-wing military dictators. For my family this seemed normal, logical. It's impossible to make up clandestine stories like those, that were carried out openly during the 1950s, 60s and 70s.

During that time most countries in South America were ruled by administrations forced upon them by the CIA, thus favored by our USA. Countries that leaned toward Socialism were considered Communist and arch enemies of conservative capitalism. The cries of "Yankee Go Home!" slowly subsided as the dictators were removed by democratic voting of the people. Interesting, as we cycled through South and Central America, we found that most elected governments were now socialistic.

Discovering Che

Setting off on our bicycles from Ushuaia in southern Argentina, we first came upon Ernesto Guevara in Cordoba, Argentina. Our meeting with him took place in the small Museo de Che.

Ernesto wasn't Cuban and as a kid he wasn't anything like the strong image portrayed on those T-shirts or that photo. In El Museo we learned that he was a sickly child. He was born in 1928 in Rosario, Argentina, into an upper-middle class family.

The eldest of four children, he was plagued with asthma. His father moved the family to Cordoba hoping the mountain air would improve his health. There, Ernesto attended elementary and high school. Later he attended the University of Buenos Aires and attained a degree in medicine. Dr. Ernesto became a dermatologist. During those formative years he also embarked on two trips. That's when he met his destiny and developed feelings about the lives and dignity of others that would lead him on a pathway toward Cuba.

Ernesto on the Move

Ernesto decided to travel through Latin America while studying medicine. Wanting to ride a bicycle yet knowing he was limited by asthma, he cleverly installed a small gasoline engine on his bike. With the power to climb hills he set off on a voyage through northern Argentina in 1950.

In January 1952, Ernesto and a friend, Alberto Granado, decided to take a year off from their studies. They rode motorcycles through South America. During those two journeys Che concluded that wealth was not equally distributed. Too many people in Argentina, Bolivia, and Peru lived in extreme poverty. A film, *The Motorcycle Diaries*, later immortalized that trip. We have cycled thousands of miles and met multitudes of people. We know how this exposure can change your life. Leaving behind a normal life, you find upon your return you're a completely different person. Experience gained through travel is "Fatal to prejudice, bigotry, and narrow-mindedness." – *Mark Twain*

Those T-Shirts, That Picture

Eventually Ernesto began to pal around with a Marxist group in Guatemala. Those rag tags were routed and he was forced to flee to Mexico. As fate would have it he fell in with a fellow named Fidel.

Deposed from Cuba, Fidel Castro was primed and ready to launch a revolution in his home land, Cuba. Ernesto had a habit of calling everyone "Che", Argentinean slang loosely meaning "pal" or "buddy". He was soon nicknamed Che.

Dear Hildita, Aleidita, Camilo, Celia y Ernesto:

If you have the opportunity of reading this letter, I will not be here any longer. You won't almost remember me and youngest members of my family won't know who I am. Your father has been a man that behaves in the same way as he thinks and, of course, he has had a firm conviction that he was always right.

Grow like authentic revolutionaries. Study all you can so as to control the technique that allows you to have a good knowledge of nature. Don't forget that the revolution is the most important cause of liberty and each of us, alone, isn't anybody. Above all: be always capable of feeling in the depths of your heart any injustice against anybody anywhere in the world. This is the most beautiful quality of a revolutionary person. See you my children. With love

Daddy.

A compelling letter from Che to his family

Che married twice. He met his first wife, Hilda Gadea in Guatemala in 1953. They married after learning she was pregnant in 1955. They had one child. The marriage ended in divorce. His second wife, Aleida March, fought beside him during the

Cuban Revolution. Married in 1959, they were together until his execution in 1967. They had four children.

Who Says You Can't Go To CUBA?

Our decision to see Cuba was originally determined in Argentina. We spent a year cycling the length of South America, Central America, and Mexico to Cancun. During those days we decided it was imperative that we *SNEAK* into Cuba to see and experience the island for ourselves. Sneak? Why not just visit? Was it against the law to travel in Cuba? NO, the ridiculous outdated rule that kept Americans away only made it unlawful to spend money in Cuba! Our ability to freely travel to Cuba was prohibited by (can you believe this?) the Trading with the Enemy Act of 1917.

*The **Trading with the Enemy Act** (TWEA) of 1917 enacted 6 October 1917, is a United States federal law to restrict trade with countries hostile to the United States. The law gives the President the power to oversee or restrict any and all trade between the United States and its enemies in times of war. In 1933, the U.S. Congress amended the Act by the passing the Emergency Banking Relief Act which extended the scope of the Trading with the Enemy Act to include any declared national emergency and not just those declared solely during times of war. The Act has been amended several other times. As of 2017, Cuba is the only country restricted under the Act.*

We questioned ourselves, "When was the USA at war with Cuba?" Did that Bay of Pigs fiasco qualify as war? We felt that was ridiculous and sounded unconstitutional. Then, as if to add insult to injury, President Bush had increased the penalty for visiting, from $100,000 per person to $250,000. WOW a potential a half million dollar fine levied against Cat and me! That only tended to whet our appetites. We *HAD* to go to Cuba. We wanted the same freedoms allowed almost all other citizens of the world. Canada and most European countries travel freely to Cuba. So, facing $500,000 fine, we decided to take the risk. We swore to each other that we would not trade with the enemy.

Could We Go Cycling in Cuba?

So, was Big Brother watching? Several friends had suggested that as soon as we posted our journal pages the U.S. government watchdogs would become attack dogs. In our opinion the entire embargo was a dinosaur left over from those commie hating days of the 1950s. The days when my John Birch Society parents thought that even Elvis Presley was a Communist plot to brainwash America's youth. Didn't our government know that Communism was dead? The fear of it, as fears usually are, had been replaced by the fear of terrorism. Were there terrorists in Cuba? That we didn't know, however, we had learned that the Cuban government provided free education, free dental and medical insurance, for all Cuban citizens. Wasn't it time to open the floodgates? Let freedom flow through free access. It wouldn't take long for things to change. We were going to Cuba. We had to go to Cuba!

Planning A Cycling Tour of Cuba

That visit to El Museo in Rosario, Argentina had begun to inspire a visit to Cuba, more than a year earlier. Our desire to cycle in Cuba had grown daily. By the time we reached Cancun, Mexico, we were determined to the point of obsession. Many days we worried about the risk of penalty. Many nights we talked about the rewards of discovery. Cuba would be opened to American tourists one day in the future. We knew when it did, that Cuba would be changed forever. Its shorelines would once again become lined with clusters of resorts like Cancun. We'd cycled through too many dangerous places in the world to turn back. Relying on our theory that 98 percent of the people in the world are good people, we decided nothing would stop us.

A Day Off In Cancun, Mexico

Our plan was to relax, lay on the beach, and enjoy a week in Cancun. The beautiful sea that we and thousands of others travel there to see was hidden by wall-to-wall condos and hotels. Our well thought-out plan of R&R was blown away by Wilma, a category 5 hurricane.

A Tough Cat, Got Nervous!

We had cycled two-thirds of the way around earth's crust including seventeen countries in Africa and the length of South and Central America and most of Mexico. During that time we'd experienced many tests of endurance and courage. We were well prepared for most hardships and dangers. Cat had endured run-ins with snakes, huge spiders, pickpockets, and even armed robbers in Peru. The hurricane had changed course and was now bearing down on Cancun. Winds in excess of 180 mph sent a chill through Cat. My idea to hunker down in a big hotel was vetoed by Cat. I'd agreed early on that if she felt threatened, the call to go or not to go was hers. She convinced me we had to get out of Cancun ASAP and get to Havana, Cuba.

Zenaide To The Rescue

Cat spotted a travel agency sporting Cubano Airline signs. The owners Martha and Carlos were experts on Cuban travel and they were *from* Cuba. However, neither spoke English and our ability with conversational Spanish was limited. As we struggled, a gal also buying tickets and speaking fluent Spanish turned and in perfect English asked, "Can I help you guys?"

Zenaide, from California, was a nanny for the rich and famous.

She was headed to Havana to meet friends. With the threat of the hurricane looming, she helped us book the next day's flight. That left us with less than twenty-four hours to pack and prepare, but then we worked best under pressure. Martha booked us and we paid and reserved Hotel Havana Libre to spend our first and last nights in Cuba. She also booked and we paid for a Comby, a van for transport from the Aero Puerto.

We went questing for plaid plastic travel bags large enough to hold our panniers. Cat easily found them, then we scurried to the Mall of the Americas searching in vain for a Cuban guide book.

Our next trip was to Wal-Mart for pasta, rice, and some freeze-dried packets of food we'd heard might be in short supply. I broke down the bikes and we packed the bags. By 7:00 pm we were set to fly. For our final capitalistic meal, we chose Argentinean parilla, a big meat barbeque. Appropriate, we thought.

Pre-Columbian Cuba

The island of Cuba was inhabited by various Mesoamerican cultures prior to the arrival of the Italian explorer Christopher Columbus in 1492. Columbus claimed Cuba as a Spanish colony.

Who Were Cuba's Original Natives?

It was estimated that up to 200,000 natives belonging to the Taino and Ciboney nations inhabited Cuba before colonization. The native Cuban Indian population were forced into reservations during the Spanish subjugation of the island of Cuba.

In 1762, Havana was briefly occupied by Great Britain before being returned to Spain in exchange for Florida. A series of rebellions during the nineteenth century failed to end Spanish rule. However the Spanish–American War resulted in Spain's withdrawal from the island in 1898 and Cuba gained formal independence in 1902.

How Did Cuba Get It's Name?

On October 28, 1492, Christopher Columbus landed in Cuba and christened it "Juana," in honor of Prince Don Juan, son of Queen Isabella. Origin's of names this far back are difficult to document, especially as most Indian tribes did not have a written language. Story has it that it's Indian name was "Cubanacan."

In the years following independence, the Cuban Republic saw significant economic development but political corruption and a succession of despotic leaders. That led to the overthrow of the dictator Fulgencio Batista by the 26th of July Movement led by Fidel and Raúl Castro during the 1959 Cuban Revolution. Cuba has since been governed as a socialist state by the Communist Party, headed by the Castro brothers. The country has been politically and economically isolated by the United States-led embargo since the Revolution.

Taking Flight In A 40 Year Old YAK

After a frantic taxi ride seeking chain lube and inner tubes, we settled for a couple of thin tubes made in Vietnam. We asked if they were strong. The clerk shrugged and said, "media fuerte." They looked thin and fragile but better than nothing. He didn't have chain lube.

9

Time was fleeting, we had to check in at the airport by 11:30 a.m. Jonathon, the bellman at our Las Margaritas Hotel, helped me get the bags and bikes down the hallway into the elevator and out the front door. Cat checked out while Jonathon helped me find a large taxi. He'd called but none seemed to be coming. Finally, in near panic, the doorman stepped into traffic and whistled. A small station wagon stopped. Tight, but we crammed in bikes, bags and our bodies. We were off without a minute to spare.

Several airport porters surged out hassling each other as we watched the spectacle. Our preference was to move our own things when possible. For us, that was safer and it saved tips. Feeling the pressure to move fast we chose a couple guys. Inside the terminal we rushed up to an empty Cubano Air counter. Martha had noted on the tickets that our flight would depart at 2:00 p.m. and we should arrive two hours early. A Cubano Air worker waved for us to come to the counter, then said, "Abierto en la hora de 12:30." All our hurry and worry was for naught.

Rick From Chicago

The good news, we were definitely first in line. At last, as other passengers began to fall in line we spotted a guy at a baggage Saran wrap machine. I wanted to have the bikes wrapped. The young guy was hesitant. Then he said, "Ees costing 120 pesos." That was about $12 U.S. I began trying to bargain but he turned and walked away. He returned with his boss, a real hard-nose. When he offered to wrap for 90 pesos I was ready to buy but then he clarified, that was for each bike. I objected and a couple of guys in the line took up our cause. When they spoke to the boss he unleashed a barrage in Spanish. One of the guys, Rick from Chicago, said, "He's bustin' their chops for trying to help you." I stood directly in front of the boss and said, "Forget it, we don't want your service." One of the guys translated as I turned away. The boss spun on his heel and disappeared into the gawking crowd.

Smoke-Filled Aisles

Rick's wife was Cuban. He traveled there often. We weren't sure what he did. It sounded like he was connected somehow to the medical profession. He said, "I hosted a group of doctors on a cycling tour around Cuba last year." His best advice, "Don't worry when the fifty-year-old Russian Yak aircraft begins to take off. The aisles will fill with what looks like smoke but it's only a cloud of condensation."

Checking in was painless except for the *painful* overweight charge of $60. No credit cards accepted, cash only, this was Cubana Air Lines. They took Mexican pesos and we were ready to fly. Argghh, we shuddered as they carelessly threw our matched set of cheap plastic luggage and the bikes onto the conveyer belt. Mexican Immigration was just a rubber stamp affair. Lucky for us, Martha had included the departure fee in the cost of the tickets.

After we were on board and seated, the flight was delayed for no apparent reason and with no explanation. We sat patiently then Rick, seated a couple rows ahead of us, said, "This is almost standard procedure." Finally we rolled back, bumped along the runway and lifted off at 3:00 pm.

As the cabin filled with condensation and our neighboring passengers eyes filled with fear, we were happy Rick had given us the heads up.

The one-hour flight was smooth as glass and crossed into an hour earlier time zone. We arrived at 5:00 pm, local. First stop Inmigracion. As we began to enter together, a man in uniform indicated each of us had to go through separately. Cat went right, I to the left. The woman in my line took my passport ran it through a computer, scanned it, then thumbed through it page by page. Next a face study. She stared at the picture, at me, then back to the picture at least half a dozen times. Finally, she stamped a separate piece of paper, in order to avoid stamping the visa into my passport. The door buzzed and opened. I spilled out into the luggage area and heard Cat banging on her door. It was stuck and she worried they were denying her admission to Cuba.

Once on the ground in Havana, we experienced a good thing about socialism. Nobody there hustled us about handling our luggage. The carts were provided and there were no porters. We were last out because we had to wait for the bikes. Special handlers brought them around to us then left abruptly without extending their hands for a tip.

Ernesto Che Guevara, MD was featured on this rare three peso note issued by the Cuban government in 1983 on the anniversary of his execution. After winning the Revolution, Che was appointed President of Banco National de Cuba. He also organized the free university system that continues to educate the people of Cuba. Che also reviewed appeals for convicted war criminals.

Chapter 2: Havana, Hurricane, and a Hasty Escape

The Cuban Money Exchange Game

At Martha's suggestion we converted U.S. dollars to Mexican pesos. Enough, we'd figured, to easily last for our planned three-week stay. You'd think changing money would be a simple thing. However it became complicated and confusing when changing Mexican pesos for CUCs (Cuban Convertible Pesos; locals called them "kooks"). The Airport Currency Exchange clerk seemed almost gleeful as he counted and recounted our pesos. Then he whipped out a small pile of kooks. I questioned the conversion rate. He said, "Mexican peso, very weak." We were happy that we were only exchanging 1000 pesos there. Their rate was one kook for 13.94 Mexican pesos. Our 1,000 pesos shrank to only 77 kooks. Holy Havana, that was more than a 20 percent discount! At that rate, we were in trouble. The only hope we had was that the exchange rate at banks would be more moderate. It was easy to figure that at that discounted rate we wouldn't have enough money to last twenty-one days.

Capitalists in a Communist Country

The next dispute should never have happened. Martha told us we'd be met by a Comby, a van. She'd said, "They will know you bring bicycles and extra bags. A man who speaks English will meet you, and accompany you to the hotel." The man, Jose, struggled with English, "You only passengers, I have small car. I am paid for only small car taxi rate. You bici y bag no feet, you must to pay more for Comby." Arguing in two different languages was futile, but we tried. I insisted he call his boss. That too went nowhere. Starving and tired of the hassle, we had him call for a van. We had already discovered that a taxi would cost ten kooks. The van driver wanted twenty. After a shouting match he agreed to fifteen and we loaded up. That comrade was definitely a capitalista!

Usually we were the center of attention when unloading our gangly bags and bikes at a nice hotel. Arriving at the Havana Libre, we were pushed aside by a French group. They were excited as they climbed into a caravan of classic cars, taking them to dinner. It was like being caught up in a 1959 Hollywood film premier. Cameras flashing and people jostling for position. This was the Cuba we were hoping to see.

The bellmen were also confirmed capitalists. They watched as we struggled to load our bags on the luggage cart, then hustled to grab them and push inside. The good news was they didn't flinch when we told them to take the bikes to the room. The Libre, long ago a Hilton Hotel, was operated by the French Melia Franchise Group.

The carpet was faded and stained, the hallways smelled of mildew. The bellman apologized as he pushed the cart to the room. Once inside, he made a big deal of demonstrating the lights and TV remote before holding his hand out for a tip. Hey, we're capitalists too, he deserved a tip. We reckoned that he had to pay the piper in order to get his elevated job with benefits. Rick mentioned that even a brain surgeon earns only $20 a month. Our two kook tip moved the bellman up to a higher income bracket.

Patience and Persistence Shall Prevail

Another test of the system, the language and Cat's ability to cope. We struggled but couldn't break the zip ties on the bikes. Cat called the front desk and asked for a knife. The girl hung up without making it clear whether they were sending one. Cat called the bellman, the same one who had just accepted the 10 percent of a brain surgeon's wages, and asked him for a knife. He said, "No."

Miffed, Cat went down to the cafeteria and asked for a knife. The waiter asked, "Why you need this?" She explained then he said, "No, knife is for eating," then turned and walked away. My turn. I called the front desk and asked the girl who spoke good English, if they had a knife we could borrow to open our bags. Time continued to tick so I called again and she said, "I have something better." Shortly, a knock on the door and there she stood, scissors in hand. Patience and persistence had prevailed.

By then it was night, a dark pitch black night. It was just 8:30, and we were starving!

That Old Sovietski Attitude

Cat called room service. The girl on the phone was curt and not helpful. Rick had warned us about employee attitude and urged us to be patient. I remembered witnessing this same attitude in 1989 while in the old Soviet Union. They were saying, "You can order only sandwich." I went down to the Italian restaurant. The waiter there said, "We have no room service!" I asked if I could place an order to go.

That caused a hubbub and the entire staff got involved. At first it was "No." Then as I whined about our hunger and the difficulties we'd endured, they weakened. They allowed two plates of pasta and a serving of bread. Wisely, we'd thrown a bottle of wine into our bags. That would definitely complement the meal.

They called, I did pickup and delivery. Dinner wasn't great but my service was sterling. The best news: we had CNN in English. Our first dose of intelligible news in two weeks.

Flying, especially in an old plane, was as demanding as cycling. Carrying our own bags, even with a little help, was tough, too. We were both bone tired.

Cat continued to stress about the situation. I told her what Vince Lombardi, former coach of the Green Bay Packers had said, "Fatigue makes cowards of us all."

Cat Hates Riding Out the Hurricane

Wilber Helps Hustle Us Out Of Havana!

We awoke to news on CNN that Cancun was being battered by the category 5 hurricane. Then really bad news for us: it was changing course and heading for Havana. Cat got nervous. I felt that if we stayed in Havana we'd at least be high and dry. She pointed out that we'd also be broke before the big breeze blew through.

The breakfast buffet was a great spread. No local comrades in the dining room, though. We assumed that type of opulence was reserved for foreign visitors loaded with plenty of kooks. A pianist served a classical mood with the food. Funny, a newspaper named GRANMA. We assumed it was a Spanish word similar to PRAVDA in the Soviet Union, which meant TRUTH in Russian.

A girl at the first desk of the travel service in the Libre lobby listened with a curious look that said, "I no understand nada." Then she called to Wilber, the guy on desk three. He spoke good English. We told him of our plan to cycle from Santiago de Cuba to Havana and our money problem. He had two pieces of bad news for us: "The exchange rate is the same, at all banks. It may be better at the money exchange, a place called Cadeca." The second news really made Cat's chin quiver, "I think all transportation, for sure trains, have suspended service, due to the coming threat of hurricane."

Good thing for us Wilber was not a quitter. He got on the phone, made several calls then said, "There is a bus to Santiago de Cuba at 3:00 today. Probably the last until after the hurricane. I have booked seats for you, okay?" Cat was thrilled, not about having to get ready to go in just a few hours, not to have to endure sixteen hours on a Cuban bus, but at riding out of Havana rather than riding out the storm. Her quivering lips broke into a giant smile, knowing we were headed out of harm's way. Cat's greatest fears had been being kidnapping and tortured. Her second and third were snakes and spiders. Now category 5 hurricanes had moved to number one on her list.

Short Of Money, No Way To Get More!

Wilber made calls and booked a Casa Particular, a B&B, in Santiago de Cuba. As he completed the paperwork and vouchers, we walked around the corner to the bank. Unfortunately he was correct, the bank rate was the same as the exchange at the airport. The 5,500 Mexican pesos that had cost almost $550 U.S. brought only a paltry 405 Cuban kooks. The embargo prohibited U.S. banks from doing business in Cuba. No bank or ATM there would recognize our credit or debit cards. We had what we had. We'd just have to stretch it, make it last.

Check that, Wilber said, "Yes, ees possible to get money, but not easy. You give me your credit card number. I send to a person in Florida, USA. He withdraws cash from card and send with another friend to Cuba. They weeel charge for service, 20 percent to withdraw and 20 percent to bring in to Cuba!"

WOW, a lot of trust and a huge discount. We chose to shoestring it on the money we had.

Fate, Wilber, and His Guidebook

Fate had always seemed to have a way of providing for us. When we asked Wilber where we might find a travel book on Cuba, he reached into his desk and pulled out a well-worn copy of a five-year-old Cuba guide book. We'd known him only for minutes yet he was willing to trust that we would return his book, worth more than a month of his wages. I wrote his name and telephone numbers inside the front cover. He knew that even if we found a copy for sale, we couldn't afford to buy it. What a guy, our first true friend in Cuba.

Wilber suggested an internet connection. He said, "They charge six kooks per hour, when the system is working." Then he shrugged. "Unfortunately, this day they are not a working day." After a wild goose chase we gave up, went back to Hotel El Libre and paid nine kooks for an hour. We had to let our family and friends know we were okay and moving out of the path of the hurricane.

Lunch was a sandwich at a little place across the street from El Libre. We shared the table with a guy from Germany. His business was industrial laundry equipment sold to laundromats and hotels. As he sipped a beer and we ate our sandwiches we wondered,

would that business be handled by a U.S. company were it not for the embargo?

We'd asked for a large car and the front desk assured us it could easily find one. With all our worldly possessions stacked on the sidewalk, we watched as the bellman blew his whistle at passing taxis. It was 1:30 pm Wilber had urged us to get to the bus terminal by 2:00. Finally a small station wagon pulled up and the bellman gestured at our pile of bags and bikes. The driver seemed ready to pull away. I jumped into the mix assuring him we could get it all on board.

As the taxi pulled away Cat asked, "Meter, use meter?"

The driver laughed as he pulled the flag down on the meter and asked, "Why do you want the meter? We call it the dog that bites you!"

Robilio, our new friend and driver, had lived in Miami. His daughter lives and teaches in San Francisco. He filled us in on sights of Havana as we drove, then helped unload at the Autobus Terminal.

16 Hours By Bus to Santiago de Cuba

Cat watched the bikes as I carried bags to the counter. Curses, they charged for excess weight. Not much, but every little kook counted. They sent the bags up a conveyor then asked me to carry the bikes out to the platform. As I emerged with my bike, a guy grabbed it from my hands and motioned for me to get Cat's. When I got back he was trying to jamb my bike into the bay upright. I screeched, he stopped, and we found a way to lay them down to avoid damage.

Tim from Chicago

While I loaded, Cat struck up a conversation with Tim, our second new friend from Chicago. He was also married to a Cuban woman. His bags were full of diapers, baby blankets, even a stroller. He was a proud new papa. Their baby boy had arrived early, while he was still in Chicago. The little guy was two months premature and weighed only two kilos. (barely more than 4 pounds) Meeting Tim on the bus was another treasure for us. He was a painting contractor from Chicago.

His wife was a Cuban pharmacist. They had applied for a visa to move her and their baby to Chicago. When we asked whether she would be allowed to leave, Tim explained, "The government provides free education but expects those who  learn to invest it in their fellow citizens. It's like the U.S. military: they'll put you through school, but you have to complete your enlistment. My wife can leave when she has finished working for another year. We plan to split our time between Chicago and Cuba.

20

We're adding a second story to the house we bought here. We will live upstairs and my mother-in-law will move in downstairs."

One effect of the revolution was brain drain. Why would a brain surgeon work for $20 a month when they could make big bucks just ninety miles away in Florida? The Castro government's free education system was sending well-trained doctors and other medical professionals to third-world countries. We'd met nurses from the U.S. in Honduras. They told us about working with skilled

Cuban doctors there. Talking with Tim was enlightening. He liked life in Cuba. Like Rick he said, "It's a great place, if you have a little money."

The modern bus was as cold as a meat locker. It departed at exactly 3:00 pm. By 6:30, we pulled in to a small station. Our driver, Emilio, announced a forty-five minute break for dinner. We walked with Tim to a fried chicken stand. He said, "My wife loves this place." They only served one greasy chicken leg to each of us, no potatoes or side dishes.

An old guy walked up, puffed his cigar, and stared over the fence. I took his photo. I loved the look, a true Cubano with hat and cigar.

We needed more food. Emilio, our impatient driver, gestured that we had to go. Then he went to bat for us with the cooks. They hustled up a couple of sandwiches.

Emilio was gunning the engine as we ran back to the bus. The sandwiches and a little leftover wine hit the spot.

Sleep was fitful at best. The seats were small and hard. It was so cold on the bus that our breath hung in the air. We asked our neighbors across the aisle to turn the air conditioning vents away from us. For warmth we pulled our jackets over our heads. Somewhere, sometime during the night, the road became bumpy, causing the bus to sway and rumble. Bus stations were strangely lit places. Good for a toilet stop but more often than not just a peek from under our jackets. How we wished we'd known about the cold. Our rain jackets and towels that would have added extra warmth, were stowed just below.

A very modern bus with very frosty air conditioning

Chapter 3: Santiago, Nellie's Casa, Fidel Takes a Beating

Arriving in Santiago at 6:50 am, Matilda and a taxi met us, thanks to Wilber. Boy, were we happy to see her! Don't know how we would have found her house. When we drug our bags and bikes out, the driver of her car, an unlicensed pirate taxi she had hired, called to a buddy. The two taxis charged eight kooks. WOW! We were going broke fast. We pulled up at a three-story house and Matilda introduced us to us to Nellie. Matilda's house just around the corner was fully booked. Nellie showed us to a bedroom without windows and a three step, step-up toilet with suicide shower. We knew well those 220 volt on-demand electric water heaters that we'd learned to cautiously use in South America. We would have loved to wash down but the electricity was out. Cold water, after freezing all night, sounded dreadful. Nellie prepared a tasty breakfast of ham and cheese sandwiches and sweet coffee. When the power failed to make its predicted return, we decided to walk into town. Smaller than Havana, Santiago had a distinctly different feeling.

The plentiful array of old cars on the streets were a photographer's dream. The buildings too, made great pictures.

Many of the old cars were pirate taxis. They all pulled up asking if we needed a ride. Hungry drivers looking for a fare. Capitalism, in a competitive market.

A small square, a restaurant with shade trees and outside food service beckoned. We tried to order Chinese. The waiter listened as we asked the size of plates and what to order. At first we decided on two plates then changed the order to one plate and fried rice. When he finally returned, food in hand, he had three plates. Way too much food. We told him we only wanted the beef dish and fried rice. He whipped out his order ticket then yelled at us. Okay, it was a language faux pas but we

felt we shared the guilt. I yelled back, then he backed off and took the pork plate back to the kitchen. When we asked for the check we apologized. He seemed to have gotten beyond the problem. Perhaps he'd sold the third dish, or eaten it. He was all smiles when we slipped him a little tip.

Nellie's power had returned. The AC felt great and we enjoyed lukewarm showers. Then we lay back and relaxed. In fact we fell into deep sleep. Strange how one can lose track of time, at times like that. We awoke in the darkened room and thought we'd slept through the night. My glow-in-the-dark watch said "5:00" we assumed a.m. Surprise, it was only dinner time.

There was a girl staying in a room down the hallway. She said, "Hello, I are Nellie's daughter," as we emerged, then turned back to her task of cleaning. Cat asked Nellie about a taxi back to town for dinner. She insisted, it was "very safe to walk." So, we were in a strange place, with a strange culture and language, and setting off in darkness. There were street lights but they were a dim yellow and poorly spaced leaving large areas of gloom. Plenty of people sat on their porches or steps. Most spoke to us with friendly voices. We never felt threatened or fearful. It reminded me of life in my old neighborhood, when I was a kid in the 1950s, in Spokane, Washington.

We beat a fast path to a pizza place we'd staked out that afternoon. Good pizza, and they had a news channel on TV. Even in Spanish it was easy to see that the hurricane had begun to loosen her grip on the Yucatan and was shifting her path toward Havana. We thanked Wilber and our lucky stars that we weren't there.

Though I felt pretty safe with the local people I suggested we taxi back to Nellie's. Cat, concerned about our finances, insisted we walk. Very dark, very safe, we felt like locals.

Preparing Bikes for Cuban Roads

We thought we'd heard someone prowling around the house during the night. No problem for us, we figured it was probably Nellie's daughter. We decided to have breakfast in. Nellie rousted her daughter Yanelis out to help. They prepared eggs, juice and coffee. Yanelis, who was nineteen, told us, "I'm going to Miami in December." I chuckled and asked, "Will you go by boat or plane?" She laughed and said, "My grandfather lives there, he entered me in

United States lotteria every year since I seven year old. This year we won." She was anxious in a nervous sort of way about going.

Her English would need to improve, but she should do well. She said, "I will work with granpapa in his grocery store."

The suicide shower always ran lukewarm. The toilet, an afterthought, was built on a step-up platform. We called it the throne room. Like so many things in extreme socialist states, it was practical. Built for utility and function, not so much for beauty.

I rode Cat's bike down the street to what Nellie called a "garage door," combination auto and bike shop. Cat's rear wheel had loosened at the axel. The mechanic wanted to take the wheel apart and check the bearings. I told him it was fairly new. So he just tightened the axel. When I asked for chain lube he handed me a can of thick black grease. I leaned the bike on the side of the garage in the shade and slathered it on.

Second trip with my bike I just oiled the chain, again in the shade. Then I remembered I should have checked the air pressure in our tires. He handed me a pump and gauge, I went to work. Sweat and work that was! I got 65 pounds pressure in 90 degrees Fahrenheit, 70 percent humidity. I rode back and rode Cat's bike back for a 65/90/80 pump, too. The guy refused to accept any money. I insisted and slipped a kook into his shirt pocket then said, "Para un cerveza."

When I rolled into Nellie's yard Cat met me with a frown. She noticed that my shorts were worn and torn from belly to butt. Nellie's next door neighbor stitched up both legs for re-enforcement and style. They looked good but didn't look like they'd last very long.

Hearing of a nearby fort we asked Nellie for directions. She yelled to a guy down the street.

Pepe, her cousin, spoke a little English. Our first need was a grocery market. He led us down the block around the corner and voila! Chilean wine a bargain at only 4.50 kooks. As we walked past a fellow with Rasta-style hair down to his knees he said, "Hello." Yes, Adriano the Rasta man spoke English. He said, "I am professor of mathematics at university." What a nice guy. He added, "I haven't cut my hair in more than ten years. And I like reggae music." Not exactly the way we'd pictured a professor in a communist country would look. Strange how all too often we're quick to pass judgment. Adriano was a very nice guy and probably a great teacher, too.

As we walked toward the store we encountered a line of people. Pepe said, "They wait to fill canisters with propane gas. Everyone use propane gas for cook. We all get free re-fill once each month."

A Castle Tour with Pepe and Jimy the Pirate

As we walked, Pepe seemed to know everybody. He said hello and shook a lot of hands. At a corner he said he'd get a taxi. We asked the price and Pepe said, "It is twenty kook." Earlier we'd talked with a couple of Dutch girls who'd mentioned they'd gone to the castle and the car cost fifteen kooks. When I told Pepe, he walked to the corner and talked with a guy in a car, a Russian-built Lada. Returning he said, "You walk around corner with me, he come get us." Intrigue? Later, we learned that the guy was an unlicensed pirate taxi. Guys like Jimy, the owner/driver take a big chance hiring out their cars, especially to foreigners. Jimy had to park out of sight down the road from the castle.

Not exactly a castle, the Lighthouse Morro Stgode was built in 1842. It was a fort clinging to a cliff overlooking the Caribbean on one side and Santiago on the other. They displayed schmaltzy-looking mannequins dressed in period costume. Pepe took Cat's sunglasses and put them on for a picture. Then he brazenly asked her, "Will you give to me these glasses?" "No," she told him, "I need them for cycling." Then he asked for my sandals.

Disappointed, he handed us off to a castle guide. Her service was included in the four kook entry fee. She pointed to pictures and repeated the written words then asked for money. We told her we appreciated her effort but would continue alone. She became surly. When we told Pepe we were disappointed that his guide service wasn't included, he stopped asking for our things.

Jimy cautiously dropped us off on a side street. Pepe told us he had an appointment. We were happy to be on our own. It was tough having a volunteer guide. He meant well but we felt he was just in our way. We'd been traveling on our own for far too long.

Fidel TAKES A BEATING

After Batista's military coup on March 10, 1952, Fidel Castro, himself just 25 years old, began to train young men to engage in the struggle along with other anti-Batista groups against what they perceived to be an illegitimate government. Ill prepared, poorly armed and trained, Fidel pilfered blue uniforms from the military hospital laundry to dress the rebels.

Castro and his men attacked The Moncada Barracks at dawn on July 26, 1953. The attack was on the day of the fiestas in Santiago. The attack began poorly. The caravan of cars carrying the men became separated. By the time they arrived at the barracks, the car with the heavy weapons had gotten lost. Lacking weapons, many of the rebels who would have taken part in the attack, were left behind. Castro drove his car into a group of soldiers at the gate. They quickly realized it was an attack. The men in the cars behind Castro jumped out believing they were inside the barracks. The alarm was sounded before the barracks had been infiltrated.

According to Fidel, that was the fatal mistake in the operation.
Fidel told of losing five, killed in the fighting and fifty-six were
executed later by the Batista regime. Eighteen rebels were
immediately executed in the Moncada small-arms target range
within two hours after the attack. Their corpses were strewn
throughout the garrison to simulate that they'd died in combat.

Thirty-four fleeing rebels captured during the next three days were
murdered after admitting their participation. A handful of rebels,
including Fidel Castro, escaped into the nearby countryside but
were quickly captured. The Santiago de Cuba Urgency Tribunal
indicted 122 defendants to stand trial for the July 26 insurrection.
Fidel received a ten-year prison sentence. His brother Raul
confessed and was sentenced to thirteen years.

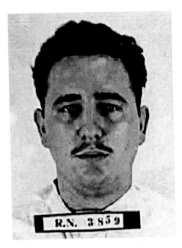

In 1954 Batista's government held presidential elections, he ran uncontested. The election was widely considered fraudulent. Some politicians urged amnesty, the Congress and Batista agreed. Backed by the U.S. and major corporations, Batista believed Castro was no longer a threat. In April 1955, after twenty-two months of confinement, Fidel and Raúl were released from prison under a general amnesty declared by Batista. Castro was twenty-nine, a recognized political figure, and the head of an organization he called the "26th of July Movement" in memory of the Moncada Assault. He soon left Cuba for Mexico to resume his revolution.

Every year since the end of Castro's revolution, the storming of the Moncada has been remembered as the "first shot" fired in the struggle against Batista.

After the revolution, in 1959, Fidel Castro personally drove the bulldozer and demolished the outer walls of the Moncada Barracks. He ordered the walls to be rebuilt in 1978.

Santiago de Cuba, The Birthplace of Revolution

Walking the streets of Santiago was a wonderful experience: our first close-up look at life in Cuba. There were lots of old trucks used as public transportation. Obviously needed, they were jammed to the rafters with Cubans headed home after a hard day's work.

Our quest for internet connection was thwarted by a lack of phone cards. The internet was operated by the telephone company. We had to buy scratch off phone cards before being assigned a computer. Unfortunately the phone company was out of phone cards.

Hungry, we found a small restaurant. Strange, they handed us a full menu then indicated they only had pasta. We ordered pasta then sat and waited and waited. The waitress seemed consumed with herself. She was walking around talking and looking at herself in a wall mirror. Giving up, we told her to cancel our order. That put things in motion, and the pasta arrived immediately. It was lukewarm, probably because she hadn't picked it up after it had been prepared. We ate!

A Sovietski Holdover

Walking back to our Casa Particular we met a young guy who spoke English. He approached and said, "I am college student, I major in language. I wants to speak with foreigners, I needs practice." We chatted small talk until he introduced himself, "My name is Vladimir. My father he speak Russian," he said with pride.

"I am name of my dad's best friend, and work comrade." A very nice young man, he walked with us pointing out things of interest in the neighborhood. Vladimir was a holdover from Cuba's Sovietski era.

Memories of the USSR. I cycled across the Soviet Union in 1989. I was the first foreigner allowed, definitely

32

the first American. An observation: many were named Vladimir. Also many named Alexander were affectionately called Sasha. My team included Dmitry and Sergei, two Sashas, and one Vladimir. All popular names from that era.

After the revolution, Cuba established diplomatic ties with the Soviet Union. Cuba became an ally of the Soviet Union during the Cold War. In 1972, Cuba joined COMECON, an organization of states designed to create cooperation among the socialist economies that were dependent upon the help and trade with the Soviet Union. The USSR and allies were important in keeping the Cuban economy afloat. COMECON and the Cuban economy went south in 1991 with the collapse of the Soviet Union, Cuba entered an era of economic hardship they called the *Special Period in Time of Peace.*

Rounding the corner to Nellie's Casa, we came upon Matilda and her husband Carlos. We stood and talked at the fence like neighbors do. Carlos asked, "Where you come from?" When we answered California, Matilda said, "California es very beeutiful, we have see of it on television."

Life there in Cuba reminded me of our simple life back in the 1950s in the U.S. Everybody in the neighborhood knew everyone else, as well as everyone else's business. There seemed to be little or no fear about robberies. All appeared to be very patriotic.

After resting and soaking up some cool air from the AC we asked Nellie about dinner. She was really happy knowing that we wanted to eat in. "I will make a nice bif stek for you." The price was extremely inexpensive, just five kooks. More than the chance to show off her culinary skills, we thought Casa Particulars paid tax on the room rent. They could serve meals without paying that tariff to the state, and they gathered the more valuable kooks.

The steak Nellie cooked was thin but tender. The rice was garnished with avocado. Pretty darned good, however, just as she served, the lights went out. Another electrical failure. Nellie said, "This happen often, but don't last long." We donned our headlamps and began eating. Pretty funny looking. Nellie laughed then brought in a battery-operated neon light.

Lightning had caused the power failure. Rain was pouring down. It was so hot inside the house that we sat on the porch soaking up the cool air and the comings and goings of the locals. They sauntered slowly, enjoying the rain and cooler humid air.

We were caught up in the tale of the hurricane. The TV news showed huge waves and strong winds pounding Havana. As the hurricane battered large parts of Cuba, we felt safe, high and dry in our little room. No electricity so no AC. It had cooled a bit but was pitch black dark, outside, and darker than dark in our room.

Cycling The Forbidden Island

Cycling the Spine of Cuba

34

Chapter 4: The Road of Revolution, Gitmo, and Cycling Cuba

We didn't know what time the power came back on. Both remember feeling the light through our eyelids for some time. We'd gone to bed in the dark and forgotten to turn off the lights. When the electricity finally returned we were staring at the bulb through closed eye lids. Despite the light incident we slept well. It was 7:00 am by the time we began dragging ourselves out of bed. Bags on bikes and in the hall, then breakfast. Yanelis said, "Luuk, I make jamon y huevos for ju." She served a sweet fruit juice followed by Cubano coffee in a small cup, loaded with sugar. Cat didn't like the strange-tasting juice. I sucked it down hoping for strength and hydration. Nellie called a friend, another Casa Particular operator in Baire, a small town 80ks from Santiago. They would save a room for us. That took a load off Cat's mind.

Goodbyes included posing in front of the house for pictures, kisses on the cheeks, and well wishes from Nellie and Yanelis. They were really sweet people. Nellie warned us again of what everyone we'd talked with in Cuba called, "Las Maestras, The Mountains of Santiago de Cuba."

Tales of the Sierra Maestre

In the autumn of 1956, a band of young adventurous revolutionaries gathered in the seaport town of Tuxpan, Veracruz, Mexico. Castro was 29, Che just 27, most of their fellow revolutionaries were so young they all wore beards to look older. They had REVOLUTION on their minds and needed a boat. They called themselves the 26th of July Movement. The Movement's name originated from Fidel Castro's failed attack on the Moncada Barracks in the Santiago de Cuba on 26 July 1953. The yacht Granma was purchased from the U.S.-based Schuylkill Products Company, Inc by a Mexico City gun dealer. He paid $15,000 U.S., money that was raised in Florida, USA, by the former Cuban President, Carlos Prío Socarrás. The name, "Granma" in English was an affectionate term for a grandmother. The yacht was said to have been named for the original owner's grandmother.

In the dark of night November 25, 1956, the yacht Granma was boarded by eighty-two youthful militants led by Fidel Castro.

Among his close followers, his brother Raul Castro, Che Guevara, and Camilo Cienfuegos, who later called themselves "los expedicionarios del yate Granma". Their destination was chosen to emulate the voyage of José Marti, the Cuban national hero who had landed in the same region in 1895 during the war of independence from Spain.

She was designed for just twelve passengers on luxury cruises.

36

Granma could be expanded to a maximum twenty-five for short cruises in ideal conditions. She was overladen, with eighty-two people, food, fuel and weapons. During the seven-day voyage in heavy seas, the leaking craft nearly capsized. Food ran short but their hunger was thwarted by sea sickness.

The landing site 175 Ks west of Bayamo, was symbolic of Cuba's long struggle. Castro chose it because it was near the area where early hero Jose Marti died in battle in 1895 during the civil war with Spain. Also, it was close to the place of Fidel's 1953 loss to Batista's army in Santiago de Cuba.

"We reached solid ground lost, stumbling along like so many shadows or ghosts marching in response to some obscure psychic impulse. We had been through seven days of constant hunger and sickness during the sea crossing, topped by three still more terrible days on land. Exactly 10 days after our departure from Mexico, during the early morning hours of December 5, following a night-long march interrupted by fainting and frequent rest periods, we reached a spot paradoxically known as Alegría de Pío (Rejoicing of the Pious)." - <u>Che Guevara</u>

The early signs were not good for the movement. They landed in daylight, were attacked by the Cuban Air Force, and suffered numerous casualties. The landing party was split into two and wandered lost for two days: most of their supplies had been abandoned where they landed. They were also betrayed by their

peasant guide in an ambush, which killed more of those who had landed. Batista mistakenly announced Fidel Castro's death at this point. Of the eighty-two who sailed aboard the Granma, only twelve of those young adventurers managed to survived.

Fidel and his fellows so revered the Yacht Granma that in tribute to her, after the Revolution, they re-named the Provencia Oriente to Provencia Granma. Also they named the official newspaper of the Cuban Central Committee "Granma".

Climbing The Tail of the Maestra

Highway 1 was a fast 5 Ks on a wide, well-surfaced road before the climb began. Yes, steep, but we wound our way up a small valley in the northeastern tail of the Sierra Maestra. It was granny gear most of the way: we had been off the bike more than a week but we managed without pushing. About half way up, a lean, muscular cyclist, Lazarus, caught us. He was riding a broken-down single-speed bicycle. No pedals, just bolts where they once were

that pressed hard against the soles of his worn-out deck shoes. He wore a tank top and his glistening arms and shoulders betrayed the effort he'd spent catching us.

Though he spoke little English, he got the point across about his hard life. He was heading to the cane fields looking for work. He rides this hill then goes to the fields every day. Stopping at the summit, after a short pigeon-Spanglish chat, we handed him our extra bottle of water. He was thrilled with his new possession, took a big swig, said, "Muchas gracias," and pedaled away in search of cane that needed cutting.

The Secret Caves of The Revolutionaries

The twelve survivors eventually regrouped in the Sierra Maestra mountain range. While Fidel Castro was setting up, "Civic Resistance" groups were formulating in the cities and putting pressure on the Batista regime. Many middle-class and professional persons flocked toward Castro and his movement. While in the Sierra Maestra mountains, the guerrilla forces attracted hundreds of Cuban volunteers and won several battles against the Cuban Army. Ernesto 'Che' Guevara was shot in the neck and chest during the fighting, but was not severely injured. (Guevara, who had studied medicine, continued to give first aid to other wounded guerrillas.) These were the opening volleys of the war, the Cuban Revolution, that continued for the next two years.

Ghastly Guantanamo

Topped out and on flat road, we were able to enjoy the countryside. It was lush and verdant. The king of Cuban crops, sugar cane, stood row upon row. We passed the crossroad to Guantanamo and paused long enough to take a photo. We have hated the way leadership back in Washington DC had been using this place as a prison. We'd began to wonder whether we hold "Enemy Combatant" prisoners there without charges because it made it difficult for protesters to get near the place. Locals told us there was an overlook but not much to see. Our decision not to venture down was that for every down, there would be an equal and opposite up.

How Did The USA Take Control of GITMO?

Guantanamo as well as all of Cuba was inhabited by Taino natives when Columbus came ashore on his second trip to the Americas in 1494. Originally called Guantánamo by the Taínos, Columbus named the bay Puerto Grande, Grand Port. During the Spanish-American War the U.S. Navy sheltered from a hurricane in the bay. The U.S. Marines landed at Guantánamo in 1898.

Following the Spanish-American War, the U.S. took control of Cuba from Spain. A perpetual lease for Guantánamo Bay was given to the U.S. for a naval station by the President of Cuba in 1903. In 1934 the Cuban-American Treaty of Relations reaffirmed the lease requiring payment of $2,000 in U.S. gold coins annually. The 1934 equivalent value of $4,085 in U.S. dollars. The lease was permanent unless both governments agreed to break it or until the U.S. abandons the property.

After the revolution, President Eisenhower insisted the lease remain unchanged despite objections from Fidel Castro. Since that time the Cuban government has cashed only one of the rent checks from the U.S. government they say due to "confusion" in the early days of the revolution, according to Castro. The remaining checks made out to "Treasurer General of the Republic of Cuba" are all held uncashed.

Guantánamo Bay was used by the U.S. as a processing center for asylum seekers and a camp for HIV-positive refugees in the 1990s. Within six months, the U.S. had interred over 30,000 Haitian refugees in Guantánamo. Since 2002 the Guantánamo Bay Naval Base, nicknamed 'Gitmo', has been used for holding high-risk detainees from the battlefields in Afghanistan and Iraq. They have been held without charges or trials. In 2009, President Obama issued orders to close Guantánamo. Congress refused to grant funds for the closure.

A Lesson in Cuban Currency and Coin

On level road, we picked up speed. We were in Palma Soriano for lunch. Asking, we got the same answers: there was only one restaurante in town. We found it and pulled the bikes inside.

The women working there were cordial, even invited us to wash our hands in the kitchen sink because the toilet didn't have running water. Everyone was casting side glances and paying attention to us. A guy came over and in Spanglish said, "Esta el primo food, a steak." It turned out to be the best and only food available. Like Nellie's, it was thin but the price was sky high.

Cheap Lunch, Worth Every Centavo and Not More

The price on the menu had us worried about our lack of funds. Thinking it was kooks we began thinking about splitting a plate. The waitress, also struggling with language, brought some coins to the table and explained, using them, that the cost was eight Cuban pesos for each plate. The exchange rate, pesos to dollars was 25 for $1.00 or for one kook. Geez, two plates of beef and rice cost only about sixty-five cents. What a deal!

Sorry, no soft drinks, they served only beer and rum. Cat chose to stick with water as she often does. I ordered a beer. Pretty good and very cheap, only forty cents. So I had three. As we chewed, (yes the steaks were tough as leather) a ten-year-old boy, Jimy, sidled up next to the table. He looked well-dressed and extremely well-fed. He spoke in halting Spanglish. We asked if he was studying. He kept a constant line of chatter going. Much of it left us guessing what he'd meant. We thought he said, "Mi padre ees living in Miami."

As we prepared to leave I suggested, "Jimy, you must read the book *Old Man and the Sea* by Ernest Hemmingway. It was written here, in Cuba!" He acted as though he didn't understand. I decided to get his address and send a copy to him when we got back home. As he began writing, a good-looking woman zipped across the room followed by a man. Both were well-dressed and sported expensive-looking watches. She helped Jimy with the address then began asking for money. I tried to explain that I would send the book for his studies. She insisted we should give money. Sorry mom, we have a family of our own to take care of. Jimy looked a bit embarrassed.

Onward through lush cornfields. Nellie's friend in Baire was expecting us. Heat and hills were grinding us down. The hills weren't humongous, it was the heat that had did us in. When we finally rolled into the town of Contramaestre we sought soft drinks. A young guy sitting drinking beers said, "Baire es diez Ks mas." Nellie had been certain there was no hotel in Contramaestre. The girl selling us soft drinks called Tu Colas told Cat, "Si es un hotel aqui, here." She pointed it out. Cat walked across while I waited and drank a second cola.

Bad news: it was Saturday night, and the hotel was completely booked. However, Wilson, a guy standing nearby and listening as Cat asked, told her he knew a place where we could stay. Cat came back, Wilson in tow. She was beyond tired and ready to call it a day. Wilson looked like a Hells Angel motorcycle gang member. Following him seemed risky. He had tattoos down both arms, but seemed honest. A Hells Angel without a motorcycle, Wilson led on his bicycle and we followed. He took us down side streets then dirt and rocky back streets. Just as we were ready to give up and turn back, he pulled up in front of a modest house. It would be our first illegal Casa Particular. We beggars couldn't be choosers; we needed shelter for the night.

Mary Lou's Clandestine Casa Particular

Wilson whispered, "Bring bicis en pronto." Cat asked, "Are we in trouble if we're caught in this Casa?" Wilson quietly told us, "Problema es para este familia, no para ustedes, you. Hurry in, ees posseeblay thees familia lose Casa." Once safely inside, Wilson introduced Mary Lou, our hostess, and the family's mom. Her husband was working in Venezuela and oldest daughter, Liza, was

living in Germany. Mary Lou was a nice gal but we were language-limited once Wilson disappeared. We felt certain he was expecting a piece of the ten kooks Mary Lou charged. She made it clear we got room only. They didn't have enough food to share. She did allow us kitchen privileges.

Mary Lou had us stow the bikes in a small room. When she opened the door to show us our bedroom we found a flood. The roof had leaked during the rain. She began mopping like

43

crazy. Short on English, she used sign language that tested our limited Spanish. We could use her shower, however hunger drove us to the kitchen first. Mopping stopped. Mary Lou seemed embarrassed, wanted to tidy up her messy kitchen. Obviously, she hadn't been expecting guests.

During mopping and cleaning, Cat and I took seats in the living room and watched Fidel Castro speak on TV, as he did every night. His speech was so similar to the one we'd seen at Nellie's that we thought it might have been taped. Funny, on the previous night we asked Nellie what he was talking about. She replied, "Minutia, esta todo minutia!"

As we watched and waited, Yanet, Mary Lou's younger daughter, came out and began applying makeup. It was Saturday night and she was goin' dancin'. Her little son Fran sat next to her then slowly worked his way onto my lap. What a polite four-year-old.

Mary Lou ran a busy house. A couple, introduced as neighbors, came in. Mary Lou cooked rice and beans for them. We got a feeling they lived upstairs. Maybe Mary Lou's tenants, we guessed they had no kitchen in their room. A few neighbors drifted through chatting with the family and checking us out. Eventually Mary Lou felt the kitchen was clean enough to use. Cat took our macaroni and cheese in and got things going. I moved the bikes into Daniel's bedroom.

Daniel was Mary Lou's nineteen-year-old son and another really great kid. He had helped with the mopping and kitchen cleaning. He and sis Yanet were headed for the Saturday night dance. While we ate they played music on a boom box and entertained us by practicing their moves. He was wearing stone-washed Levis and a T-shirt. Yanet made her entry wearing a skin-tight, striped orange dress. With a CD blaring from their ghetto blaster, they began to gyrate. It was a wonderful, family-feeling experience for us. We sensed they felt the same. It was just a typical Saturday night like in places all over the world. Young people all love the same things, everywhere.

It was the end of a very tiring and interesting day. We finished our food as the dancers exited. Then we snuggled under the fresh sheets on Mary Lou's bed.

On the Road to Bayamo, 48 Ks

Strange how we'd began to feel a part of Mary Lou's family. Still tired, we laid in until we heard the rattle of pots and pans. When we stepped out of her bedroom, Mary Lou motioned for us to sit at the table. Surprise! She'd prepared a scrumptious spread of eggs, bread, and coffee. When I asked, "Cuanto?" how much, she shook her head, "Nada," nothing. We had expected to pay our way. Cat quietly left an additional two kooks on the table. Mary Lou silently accepted.

She and Fran, the only ones awake at 8:00, went out front, cautiously looked both ways, then waved for us to exit. Hugs and a short goodbye and we bumped off down the dirt street with that old familiar melancholy feeling.

A Foreigner Moment

A line of people stood staring into a store window. There was a customer inside talking with the clerk. The next in line told us we should wait five minutes. We stood as the one inside picked up a few items then checked out. As he exited Mr. Next in Line was allowed in. He too, found a couple of things and paid. Then an embarrassing moment: as the clerk let him out, he motioned for us to come in, bypassing the rest of the line. They all seemed okay with it. One couple smiled and waved us in. The clerk locked the door behind us. We got bottled drinking water and paid. The clerk then opened the door again and ushered us out. Was this strange procedure for security? Everyone we'd met stressed how safe it was in Cuba. This looked a bit suspect. Perhaps because it was a CUC-

only store that differentiated us from those dealing in pesos.

The road was flat, so we pedaled hard and fast. Cycling just the short distance of 48 Ks to Bayamo had us there in less than three hours. Then came the search for lodging. Wilber's Lonely Planet listed several. Hotel Telegraph was our first choice. They had rooms without TVs and with fans only, no air conditioning. Onward to what the book described as the best value in town. Hotel Royalton had recently been renovated. They showed us a couple of room choices. The one on the third floor had a plaza view. They had no rooms on the first floor and there was no elevator. We took the plaza view. We were allowed to store the

bikes in an office where they kept their computer and TV equipment. The very best thing was the rate: twenty-four kooks.

Cyclists Rene and Susaune from Germany

An air-conditioned room and hot water, what a treat. We cleaned up then headed out for lunch. Another treat, the hotel had a wonderful restaurant. Good food reasonably priced. After lunch we went searching for a super-market and internet shop. Found both but unfortunately they were closed. Very few shops were open on Sunday.

We spotted another cycle touring couple, a couple of blocks away. Hustling, we caught them at their Casa Particular. Rene and Susaune were hot and tired because they'd ridden in from Holguin. Susaune said, "It is not such a long ride but it is a lot of up-hills and from winter headwinds." Rene added, "It is our first day cycling. We flew away from Germany and into Cuba just yesterday. We are jet lagged, too." They were anxious to get some rest and cold showers. We made a date to meet later at our hotel.

Walking around was like being caught inside a time-warp. Old cars were plentiful. Old folks sat and chatted in the music filled plaza. A strange fellow scoot-stepped across the marble surface in time with the music. Slithering directly up to our camera lens, he reminded us of some of the more interesting people, groupies, that had followed our band *Acadiana* back home.

Wine Smuggled From a Spanish Restaurant

Back at Hotel Telegraph we asked and voila! They programmed

CNN in English on our TV. We caught up on all the latest news. I rested while Cat went on a wine safari. The girl at the front desk had told us of a place that had white wine. Interesting story, Cat found the place, a Spanish restaurant. The waiter said, "You aren't allowed to come in wearing shorts." After a look at the menu she said, "Not a problem, gracias." The prices were too high and as in Spain, they didn't start serving until late. They did have a couple of bottles of white Spanish table wine. She asked about buying to take it away. The waiter shrugged at first then pointed across the street. Muy interestante, Cat walked across and waited. Soon he came across with the two bottles in a bag and collected the money. The price was about the same as it would have been in a store. Contraband wine, for us a very good deal!

Dinner downstairs was a little disappointing, pasta with a strange-tasting sauce. The wine was fine, not great, but way ahead of having none. As we ate Rene and Susaune joined us. They'd already had dinner at their Casa Particular but enjoyed a couple of beers while telling us of their plans. They had a month to cycle. A couple of weeks in Cuba and a couple in Mexico. They had previously visited Cuba but by bus not bicycles. They'd gone cycle touring in other worldly places. We enjoyed sharing stories of the road. We reminisced about our ride through wintery weather in Russia and spring breaking out in Poland and Germany. That was just a scant eighteen months back. We'd come a long way, BABY!

CNN ran more of the same old evening news. We'd decided that if you miss a few days of CNN, like a soap opera, in a day or two you can pick right up where you left off.

Bayamo to Las Tunas, 82 Ks

Our included breakfast was tasty. I brought the bags down and loaded the bikes. Cat went searching for money. On the trek she ran into Rene and Susaune involved in the same hunt. The bank didn't have money to change and sent them to the Cadeca, the local money exchange office. They had kooks but were uncertain about changing Mexican pesos, a very slow process.

I was beginning to worry about Cat. It was 10:00 by the time she got back. It made for a late start on a hot and windy day down a narrow road. The village of Cauto was about halfway to Las Tunas and we were hungry. The first place we found sold only soft ice cream cones for one peso, about five cents. We each wolfed down a couple of them and wanted more but held off for more substantial food.

Then, we found a bakery that wouldn't sell us bread. A gal in line there, Mary, got four rolls and handed them to Cat. When we tried to pay, Mary refused. I pulled out the camera to memorialize the moment. The gal and a guy in the little window said something. We figured they wanted a picture, too.

Somehow, they got the point across that they had given us the bread. It was for selling to locals only. Milda and Juan, the one-armed baker, handed us a handful of rolls. What kind and generous people. Well, the bread was Cuban property and they were Cubans citizens!

There was a row of food booths across the street. We were nervous about street food so walked on to what they called a grocery store. It was a temporary metal building. Unfortunately it was closed until 1:30. We sat in the shade and waited patiently. As

the time to open neared, a small crowd gathered. Cat waited her turn then bought two Tu Colas. They were operating a grocery store with empty shelves.

Back to the roadside stands. I stood the guard with the bikes while Cat sought food. Upon returning she was pretty excited. She'd found two pieces of folded pizza. She described the process. The guy puts dough in a black iron skillet, smears a little sauce on top, then puts them in a homemade wood-burning oven. Once cooked, he handed them to Cat on a bit of cardboard. They were delicious and cost only four pesos, or twenty cents each.

We sat on the bank of a muddy creek and watched a fisherman haul out a big one while enjoying our pizza feast. What a find! We hoped this entrepreneurial enterprise had caught on and would spread those tasty morsels to every town we'd pass through.

The road took a turn for the better and we found ourselves zipping along with a brisk tailwind. We swept into Las Tunas before 3:00 pm. Hotel Las Tunas was not on the highway. Lost, we asked, then had to backtrack up a long, slow hill. The hotel sat atop like the Parthenon.

No Elevator and No Wine In The Inn

The hotel was imposing in a Sovietski sort of way. Big box function without flare. The good news? They had a room. Then the bad news came in bunches. The elevator was out of service, and our room was on the fifth floor, and worst of all, they had no wine.

Then a bit of good news: they were working on the lift and would have it operating soon.

We settled at a table in the lobby and sipped beers while waiting. After a couple brews each, the security guy came running to tell us that we could take the bikes up. The asensor (elevator) rattled and jerked but it worked. With the bikes stored in our room we took luxurious showers. They'd told us there would be hot water, but lukewarm was all that made it as high as the fifth floor. We had a view of a beautiful, almost underused, swimming pool.

Dinner downstairs was another Sovietski-style experience. People stood in line waiting to be seated. We took a place at the back of the line. A waiter came to the door and motioned to us. Another rather embarrassing moment until we realized the others were a group. The small table he gave us was directly under an AC vent that was blowing like an arctic hurricane.

Dinner was good. Pork for Cat and a steak with rice for me. They found a bottle of Cuban white wine. It looked like a Riesling bottle but was so sweet we had a tough time drinking it, but did our best. Even bad wine was okay at times like that.

TV was limited to a few Spanish-only stations. Yes, they were broadcasting Fidel Castro and Hugo Chavez, telling it like it was. We went directly to bed and sleep.

A Day of Rest in Hotel Las Tunas

Included breakfast was at best fair, to say the least. Juice, eggs and bread. Funny, we had always thought of Cuba as a coffee and bread country. All we'd had thus far had been second rate. Oh, the bread was just plain white like Wonder Bread and not even toasted.

A Pedicab Ride with Geovanny

Downtown was quite a distance from the hotel. The desk clerk suggested a pedicab and hailed one for us. Our pedaler, Geovanny, was new to the job and wasn't strong enough, yet. And, being only his third day he hadn't learned where places were located. That left us going in circles and ask, ask, asking. We wanted to find the telephone company to call our friend Tim, the guy we'd met on the bus. Our hope was we could connect to let him know that we were coming to Camaguey and

wanted to meet his little family. Also, we wanted to use the phone company internet.

We spotted the tower with the microwave dishes but Geovanny had a mind of his own. So, after quite a few times around several different blocks, he asked another driver who led us in.

This Etacsa Telephone office had only one computer. While

waiting, we tried the phone number Tim had given us. It took the advice of several people to finally figure out which phone card we would need. Then, which phone to use. Finally, we connected with his mother-in-law who spoke no English. We asked, in Spanglish, for her to let him know that we'd be in Camaguey in three days.

As we checked e-mail messages, a Canadian guy stepped inside, sighed, and asked how long we would be. We had a few more minutes to go answering family messages. A couple of young girls seated next to us spoke up in English, "We only needed about fifteen minutes." They were from the Caribbean Island of St. Lucia. The Canadian guy asked if they were students. "Yes, medical students." He said, "A lot of young people come to Cuba to study medicine. The university has a great medical teaching program and it costs a lot less than most in Western countries."

The Search for Cash, Banks Closed, Power Outage

Our next quest for money was thwarted by a power outage. There were several banks along one street. None were open. We didn't understand until a guard got the point across: "No electricity." He pointed down the street and said, "el signo azul," the blue sign. We could only guess that the power grid started and stopped at that point or they had a generator. At any rate, regardless of the low rate, we got no money. They refused to change our Mexican pesos at the only operating bank in town.

The grocery store we found had electricity and a few things on the shelves. With a bottle of cheap Chilean white wine and two mineral waters, we set off walking back up the hill. Too far and too hot. A couple of pedicabs were tailing us. We gave in and chose one. He was a husky guy and took to the hill with gusto. As we neared the hotel, he stopped and pointed to a trail up a dirt bank. He was telling us to walk. Slightly disgusted, we told him we expected to pay less. Remembering Rick's advice that a brain surgeon only made twenty dollars per month, the two kooks he wanted to charge seemed excessive. Especially if he wouldn't or couldn't go the distance. The thought of a discount brought new inspiration to his brainy, brawny, cyclists legs. He pulled around the corner and easily pumped up the steep driveway.

We got a couple of ham and cheese sandwiches from the restaurant. They are the most tasty dietary staples in Cuba. We ate in the room and spent the rest of the afternoon resting.

Dinner down, and it was okay. Chicken for Cat, and for me, a pork chop.

Las Tunas to Sibanico, 82 Ks

Breakfast was the usual fare served with the usual flare by girls who seem disconnected and distant from their task at hand. Bikes packed, we brought them down one at a time in the now-functioning elevator. Out the door and down the drive. We got a pic of the hotel then Cat posed in front of the giant Memorial to Independence across the street.

Fearing running out of kooks, we cycled back into town and resumed our quest. The first bank we came upon and the Cadeca were still dark. Third time was the charm: we got cash and were off by 10:00 am.

Hit a Cyclist, Go to Jail

Though the road was narrow it was flat and fast. Drivers of trucks, buses, and cars were all very cautious and courteous. We'd heard that if a vehicle hits a cyclist it was automatically the driver's fault. We liked that law. Codified or not, drivers seemed to observe it. Why not have a law like that everywhere?

Lunch was at Hotel Guaimaro, a rundown place in a small town. It was teeming with students there on what they called a "Social Event." They wore the red uniforms with pride but acted like young people everywhere. They joked and laughed in Spanish, about us, we thought.

When I took the camera out, several acted camera shy and scampered. One couple, a handsome boy and cute girl, liked the picture I took of them. As we handed out our cards the teacher walked up and grabbed one from the hand of a girl, read it, then handed it back to me. He indicated he didn't want us to pass them out. I asked, "Why? We're just two people, husband and wife traveling around the world on bicycles." I struggled to get my question across in Spanish. As I tried to explain I handed one to another student. He turned and sulked away.

The cafe waitress told us that they had no chicken but then delivered fried chicken legs, rice, and beans. We had to fetch soft drinks from our bags because they only offered rum and beer.

We thought about calling it a day and staying there. After seeing a room in the Guaimaro hotel, we chose to move on. It was hot and a long way to Camaguey, too far to make that afternoon. Plugging along we rolled into a tiny pueblo, Sibanico. There was a small hotel not much better than the Guaimaro but, by then we were tired and worn down. They had a room. It wasn't ready so we'd have to wait an hour.

The patio behind the hotel was full of Etacsa Telephone Company workers. They were sipping beers, laughing and joking. Why not join them? What better way to spend an hour wait? The girl offered two kinds of beer: a local and Crystal. The local was favored by the workers and for good reason. Crystal cost one kook, the local ten pesos about twenty-five cents U.S. We chose local, too.

Dr Jorge, Gilberto, Pedro, Norge
The Best Cheese In The World and Company Pride In Cuba

The phone company guys drifted out and were replaced by a group of four others. They too were laughing and enjoying a real happy hour. One, Jorge, spoke some English. He was a doctor.

The others Gilberto, Pedro, and Norge worked at a nearby cheese factory. They said they made the best cheese in the world. With a little urging from Dr. Jorge, Pedro ran across and brought a wheel of it for us. Although it was government-owned, those guys had as much if not more pride in their product than any corporate workers could or would. In one of the pictures we took, Norge was looking longingly at the female desk clerk. That caused a stir because she was Gilberto's girlfriend. That resulted in a bit of fun, wheedling, and lots of laughs.

Charles (Atlas) Carried the Bikes Up to a Muy Malo Room

The desk clerk introduced us to Charles the hotel manager. Apparently she had been waiting for his approval to allow us a room. He spoke even better English than Dr. Jorge. He took Cat up to see the room. She reported back, "Very basic but two rooms, one for the bikes." When we told Charles we would take the bikes to our room he introduced his security officer. He was adamant we should leave them down, he would watch them. He wanted to keep them in a room near the desk, that didn't have a door. We explained

to Charles we had our clothing in the bags and absolutely wanted them with us, he explained to the security guy then got behind me as I struggled and helped me lift my bike up the stairs. Then Charles carried Cat's bike up under one arm. I called him Charles Atlas. He knew about Charles Atlas and explained to the others. Another laugh. A lot of laughing going on, maybe the result of the world's best cheese and cheap local beers.

Everyone Owns Everything!

The shower was a hose dangling into a bucket. The water was cold, icy cold. We took a vote and decided to go to dinner first. We were in a suite of sorts. The first room was a living room, however the furnishings, save a couple of broken tables, had long ago disappeared. The bedroom was just a bed. A list of furnishings on the back of the door teased us with things that once were. A TV, chairs, and a refrigerator. Like my experience in Russia in 1989, I observed some of the comrades stealing from themselves. That is, if you buy into the theory that everyone owns everything.

Showing absolutely no willpower, we cut the wheel of cheese open and gorged on it. Best in the world? For sure the best in Cuba!

Dinner with another room full of workers. Another group of telephone guys drinking, eating, and laughing. So much like the camaraderie between workers I'd known in my younger years as a meat cutter with supermarkets. The food being served looked good. We tried to order the same dish the guys were having. The waitress let us know they only had enough for the workers. Let's assume that they weren't being prejudiced. Perhaps the workers had ordered in advance. At any rate, we got only a few pieces of boney ham on rice and beans. Oh, they did find a bottle of white wine, the same Chilean we'd had before. And it tasted even better, priced at only three kooks.

The shower head hanging down on the hose still ran cold only! We managed spit baths. Then, remaining road grime and sweat aside, we were so tired that sleep came easily.

Sibanico to Camaguey, 45 Ks

Nobody was stirring in that inn that morning. The clerk told us they didn't serve breakfast but we'd find food in the pueblo. Taking the bikes downstairs was much easier than what Charles Atlas had endured.

Finding food wasn't easy. There were a couple of cafés but they had only soft drinks or beer, no food. Each place pointed and promised we'd find food further down the road. At the point of giving up, we found a sandwich place. The food of choice, the only choice they had: ham sandwich. No complaint, they were very tasty. Perhaps partially due to our hunger. They were larger than those at the hotel and the cost was less. The women offered only ham *or* cheese. We asked for a combo, so she took the cheese out of a cheese sandwich and put it on our ham. Get beyond the limited choice and imagine, those great tasting morsels cost only four pesos or twenty cents each. The only drink available was a cloudy-looking fruit and rum punch. We opted for our onboard lemon lime drink. Rum for breakfast, no wonder those Cubanos laughed so much!

Rum Contributes to Cuban and U.S. History

Facundo Bacardí Massó, the founder of Bacardi, moved to Cuba from Spain. In 1862 he opened a distillery in the city Santiago de Cuba where he produced a rum that stood out for its taste and purity.

Rum was popular in Colonial America and it was one of the rum distillers largest markets. Rum was one of the ways the colonialists separated themselves from gin-drinking Brits. And because of the technical know-how present in New England, much of the world's rum was made in distilleries there. Unlike Europe, colonialists didn't care for powdered sugar. So the theory goes that the colonial love of rum and the rum industry contributed to the American revolution.

Chapter 5: Cuban Bride, Baby, Church, and Camilo

Marc's Young Bride, Her Mom, and Mom's Young Boyfriend

With only a short distance to cycle, we rolled through the countryside at a rapid pace. Our only stop for a soft drink was a steep climb to a restaurant above the highway. A group of people were also taking a break from driving. Marc was from Paris, France. His wife Elizabeth, was Cuban. They'd met at a party during a game played by the revelers. Seems that he and Elizabeth were born on the same day, twenty years apart. Game rules required they dance together. That was the beginning of a global romance. Spring and autumn romances seemed to run in Elizabeth's family. Her mom Digna's boyfriend, Machi, looked about the same age difference, in reverse.

Elizabeth had moved to Paris with Marc after the wedding. Homesick, she flew back to mama's arms. She'd been back in Cuba for two months. He was there to convince her to return to Paris. They were going to lunch at her nearby uncle's home. A going-away party for Elizabeth.

They were in a car. Cat asked if they owned it. Marc explained, "Eet belong to the Cuban government and company Machi works with. Eet illegal for me to be ride with him. I must duck down under window as we pass through roadblock." As in all crimes regarding foreigners in Cuba, there would be no penalty to Marc if caught. However, Machi could lose his job and license to drive. Well, if we think about someone taking a company car on an unauthorized trip with other than employees, back home in California, they'd probably lose their job, too.

Wilber's Lonely Planet guidebook told us that the best hotel in Camaguey was the Gran. After last night we needed a little pampering. Angling through the streets we were soon lost. As we studied the map a young guy cycled up and offered a room at a Casa Particular. We waved him off and told him we were going to the Hotel Gran. We thought we had the directions but he urged us to follow him around the corner. He seemed happy to be helping and was quite pleasant. Several turns through the narrow streets and then we saw the hotel sign. Suddenly, he was more interested in money than friendship. I pulled out one of our WR 2 cards and handed it to him. He expressed dismay but lost our attention as a familiar voice called out, "Hey, Pat and Cat!"

Good Fortune Delivers Tim to Us

Fate often has had a way of providing for us. It was our friend Tim. You remember Tim from the bus. How could that be in a city of 750,000 people? He couldn't have known we were coming to the Hotel Gran. Unbelievably, he was out spending the afternoon  looking for a five liter bottle of water and toilet paper. Two things he said that were in desperate short supply.

His wife and new baby, Clayton Ander, were still in the hospital. He was in a hurry to get back because he also had food for them. He said, "The hospital food is terrible, but then isn't that true back home, too?" Before he hurried off he said, "I'll try to join you for dinner tonight."

The Gran Hotel was a splurge. The bonus was that they received CNN in English. They also had an elevator and allowed our bikes into the room. The good news ended there. When we jumped in to our badly needed showers, there was no hot water. At

first they told us it would come on at 4:00 pm. Cat went on a pizza safari and scored. Double the cost of those in the countryside, yet still great tasting as well as a bargain at forty cents each.

Thirsty, I went to the restaurant for soft drinks. The price surprised me and my wallet. I came up short, but Maria the bartender solved the problem from her own purse. I told her I'd go to the room for more money. She said, "I leave now, I come back here for work desayuno, breakfast." When I promised to repay she smiled and shrugged. "No es importante." Well, she did get as much in tips as a brain surgeon earns in a day.

Hot water at 4:00 on floor four didn't happen. We ran it for a long time as they had suggested then we called and they sent a plumber. He fiddled with the controls and left. They finally called to say there was a problem. Damn! Pay the big bucks only to have them splash cold water on us.

A little walk around as we sought a place to change money, then another disappointment. We had to wait in line with the locals for twenty minutes. Once ushered inside the bank we had to sit and wait some more. At last, our turn. The guy took our handful of Mexican pesos gave them the typical thorough inspection then rejected one. A 500 peso note dated May, 1995. He tried to explain that they weren't allowed to take 500 peso notes of that date. Our only fear was counterfeit. We were so short of funds that losing forty kooks could mean the difference between eating and not, or worse, eating without wine!!! He counted out the kooks and slipped them across his counter then pushed the bad peso note back. The good news? He didn't confiscate it.

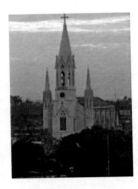

Rain began to spatter down as we found the telephone/internet shop. Messages from home were all good news. After answering all, we emerged an hour later and it was pouring down. We dashed through the streets, our hotel umbrella held high.

Dinner and a sunset view from the top-floor restaurant. Veal, and it was good, expensive, but good. In a country where food wasn't abundant, whether socialist or capitalist, you must pay the freight. We did talk briefly with a group from Holland there on a scuba diving excursion. Tim was a no-show. We figured he was tied up at the hospital. We were delighted for him. He was so happy and caught up with his little Clayton. Okay too, for us, we definitely wanted to move on early en la mañana.

CNN and early to bed.

Camaguey to Ciego de Avila, 114 Ks

A buffet breakfast short on variety but plenty of the few items they did have. As promised, Maria was there. I took pictures of the sunrise and one of her. When we were finished we called her over and handed her a generous tip that included the return of her investment for our soft drinks. Aren't people nice?

Godless Commies?

An observation, one photo taken from our hotel captured a Catholic church. A beautiful pre-revolutionary building covered in scaffolding. This meant that the work was being completed by the Cuban government. There were no private contractors. A little-known fact back home is that in this GODLESS COMMUNIST enclave more than forty percent of citizens were practicing Catholics!

Who Was Camilo Cienfuegos?

Down and out early, we found ourselves amidst traffic ranging from horse and buggy to trucks and buses. Then we came upon a long line of school kids carrying a banner. They waved and shouted to us then stood on a bridge and threw flowers into the river below. We learned later that it was Camilo Cienfuegos's birthday. Following his death, each year on his birthday students began throwing flowers into the sea near the crash site. The tradition had grown into a national holiday. Kids everywhere were throwing flowers into water, here a river, in his memory.

Camilo Joins The Revolution

Camilo went from Cuba to New York, and from there to Mexico, where he met with Fidel Castro. Camilo Cienfuegos (1932-1959) was a leading figure of the Cuban Revolution, along with Fidel Castro and Ché Guevara.

Camilo was one of 82 rebels packed into the 12-passenger yacht Granma, which left Mexico on November 25, 1956, arriving in Cuba a week later. As one of the survivors of the Granma group, Camilo had a certain prestige with Fidel Castro that the others who joined the revolution later did not.

By the middle of 1957, he had been promoted to Comandante. In 1958, the tide began to turn in favor of the rebels, and he lead one of three columns to attack the city of Santa Clara; another was

commanded by Ché Guevara. One squad was ambushed and wiped out, but Ché and Camilo converged on Santa Clara.

Camilo's force reached the army garrison at Yaguajay in December of 1958. There were about 250 soldiers inside. Camilo attacked the garrison but was repeatedly driven back. Eventually, the garrison ran out of food and ammunition and surrendered.

The handsome, affable Camilo was very popular, and upon the success of the revolution was probably the third most powerful man in Cuba, after Fidel and Raúl Castro. He was promoted to head of the Cuban armed forces in early 1959.

On the night of October 28, while flying from Camaguey to Havana, Camilo's plane disappeared. No trace of Camilo or the airplane was ever found. Cienfuegos' disappearance remains unexplained. There is some debate in regard to Cienfuegos death, although Cuban government approved historians do not believe that there was any foul play by the government. Source, *Thoughtco.com*

Chapter 6: Lenin, Che, Fidel and Communism

We spotted a picture of V. I. Lenin on a billboard, then one of Che and Fidel on a nearby building. According to what we'd read,

Fidel wasn't a communist initially. A socialist yes, but not a commie. He wanted to ally with the U.S. however, President Eisenhower avoided meeting him. He relegated that chore to V.P. Richard Nixon. Nixon had already branded Fidel a Communist back when Communism held the greatest loathing and fear among Americans.

Was Che a Communist?

According to historian and author Jon Lee Anderson, "Che was a revolutionary socialist. He wondered what it was about Che that made him so susceptible to being turned into a harmless, though profitable icon. The qualities which his admirers cite are well-known. Physical bravery, self-sacrifice, asceticism, and giving his life for a cause."

A careful review of Che's career demonstrates that his political conceptions had nothing to do with Marxism and that the panaceas

of armed struggle and guerrilla warfare with which he was identified were fundamentally hostile to the Revolutionary Socialist struggle of the working class."

Our feeling is that Che was a SOLDIER. He was driven by his inner feelings of a need to help lift the poor out of abject poverty. Remember, these feelings were developed during his bicycle and motorcycle tours in South America. We can relate to his way of thinking. It's easy to understand when you've been face-to-face with those deprived conditions. We have seen, witnessed, and been immersed in those same conditions from the perspective of our bicycle seats. There is no better way to see, experience, live, or love the world than from a bicycle. The risks are well worth the rewards!

Che always seemed most at ease in battle fatigues

Chapter 7: Cheese, Pizza, Song and Dance, and Victory!

Pedaling along at a good pace we were overtaken by a young guy in cycling clothes. Reynaldo, a Cuban National Bicycle Champion, was so intrigued by us that he slowed his pace and led us into his hometown of Florida. We stopped and bought three colas, then sat together  attempting to communicate. From what we got in the fractured conversation, he was a team racer who'd just turned thirty. He wanted badly for us to visit his home and have lunch there. It was a long way to Ciego and way too early for lunch.

Fabulous '57 Chevy

Back when I began to accumulate real estate properties, I always had a philosophy to never fall in love with inanimate objects. However, as I aged I had a hard time maintaining that attitude regarding classic cars. Cuba was famous for them and they were everywhere. My love of old  iron had us stopping often and wheeling out the camera. I graduated from high school in 1957 and always dreamed of going to my fiftieth class reunion driving a '57 Chevy. Here they had no idea what the value of their classics would be in the USA. Owning a '57 was way beyond budget for me. We decided that perhaps we'd just cycle to that event!

Leaving our hotel, I spotted an open garage door. Inside was a beautiful '57 Chevy convertible. It was enshrouded in clear plastic wrapping. As I stepped in a guy rose up from the behind it and asked in Spanish, "Que pasa?" Using my best Spanglish I got the point across that his car was worth a lot of U.S. dollars. He just shrugged as if to say, "What good does that do me?"

Another Pair of Road Warriors

Rolling along we caught sight of cycles coming our way. They were road warriors riding fully loaded. Hard to believe that Robert and Ida were from Holland. They were riding during the first week of a month long journey. We stood and chatted comparing notes about places we'd all visited. Time was fleeting, they had a ways to go and so did we. A moment together, then we were off in opposite directions.

Pizza and Marcos For Lunch

Finally escaping traffic, we were in countryside. Another day of good highway and friendly drivers. As we rolled into a tiny crossroads called Pueblo, a guy called out for us to stop. Hungry, we took his advice. We thought he probably owned or was related

to the owner of the little cafe he stood in front of. Good news? The place had one of those ovens and the smell of pizza hung thick in the air.

Marcos, the guy waving said, "I have business, selling cheese beside the road." The pizza was great,

71

hot and cheap. Marcos found ways to communicate the fact that he was in a private business. We'd seen guys like him holding up wheels of white cheese calling out to passing cars and trucks. Marcos and small cafes serving the wonderful pizza may just have been the beginnings of private enterprise.

Onward with full stomachs and new friends, we raced with cowboys on horseback for a while. The lead caballero was asking something and pointing to his wrist. I thought he wanted to know the time. When I shouted out "tres y media" 3:30, he shouted again. We began to think he was asking me to give him my watch. He stayed with us for about half a kilometer then his one-horsepower machine gave up, it was no match for our powerful legs.

No Room In The Inn, Then a Five Story Walk Up

As we pulled into Ciego de Avila, it began to rain. We'd decided to find Hotel Ciego de Avila. The guidebook described it as modern. Rain was pouring down as we rode into the entry drive and saw an almost exact copy of the Sovietski-styled Hotel Las Tunas. It was too wet and too late to go hotel hunting, we would stay. Well that was, we wanted to stay. After waiting my turn in line for almost thirty minutes the desk clerk said "Sorry no rooms." I couldn't believe it. I stood dripping and whining, "You must have a room, where shall we go? What shall we do?" He picked up the telephone and called another hotel. They too, were fully booked. Another call brought the same result.

We were getting very worried and asked if he knew of a Casa Particular. He held up his index finger and signaled for me to wait. He flipped through his book found a blank line for today and asked when we will leave. "Manana," I said. "At what time do you leave?" "8:00 am," I said with a shiver. He marked out the vacant line. We had a dry place for the evening. We felt that they blocked the room for both days to keep from double booking. We were so happy that leaving the bikes in his office and carrying our bags up five flights seemed a small burden. Room # 519 in Hotel Ciego de Avila was also a carbon Sovietski copy of Hotel Las Tunas: the rooms were identical.

Cat scored their last bottle of white wine. We sipped in our room as we showered and dressed. Dinner in the hotel restaurant. The food portions seemed to be getting smaller, or was it that our appetites were growing larger? Pork parmesan was a small piece of pounded pork topped by processed cheese with rice and potatoes. To fill our hungry bodies required an extra order of potatoes. We added a couple glasses of red wine for flavor. The service was the slow and slipshod style that we'd become accustomed to.

Wondering how locals could afford the place, we began to watch as they ate and paid. They all had chits, papers that they handed to the servers when finished. Were they allowed free hotel rooms for vacations? The hotel wasn't exactly a resort. The large swimming pool had been drained. However, when you work all year and get a free vacation, it may seem like a wonderful experience. I told Cat that I'd seen this same treatment for workers in the Soviet Union.

Ciego de Avila to Sancti Spiritus, 85 Ks

Breakfast was worse than the dinner food. Greasy eggs and bread rolls. No juice, just a weak cup of coffee. We asked the desk to book us at the Hotel Sancti Spiritus. The young desk clerk called then said, "They have rooms, they are a bit out of town." We preferred being in town so he called Hotel Rancho Hutuey and said, "I have booked a room for you." When we paid the bill he'd added two kooks for the calls.

The road was rural and bumpy. We stopped in Jatibonico for lunch. The restaurant with a sign for pizza was unfriendly, they turned us away. The waiter said, "Come back in one hour." A woman standing nearby said, "There is no other pizza in town." (Obviously, it was a government-operated restaurant.) At a cafeteria down the street, a friendlier lady informed us that they were out of food, then pointed across the street. A wonderful street merchant had a little box stove and was cooking that really good pizza. I went across to Oro Negro Service Station for soft drinks. We sat on a little wall watching locals watch us. A truck full of cabbage pulled in. The nice gal from the cafeteria ran across and got two heads. She now had at least some food. Then a guy working with the pizza man also ran. More memories of the Soviet Union and cabbage soup.

We rode through Sancti then pulled up a hill and out of town following the directions given by several nice people. Finally we found Hotel Rancho Hutuey, only to be told they were fully booked. We began to complain. I told them about the call and reservation we'd made that morning. A fellow standing nearby, Alfredo, signaled for us to wait. The clerk hemmed and hawed then finally told us we had room, number 415, a cottage, up the hill and away from the restaurant. The rate was 55 kooks, about $66 U.S. High, but then it was a room and it did include breakfast.

Pushing out of the reception area, we ran into a group of Brits. Several asked questions and wanted to talk. We answered as best we could but were eager to get to a hot shower.

Alfredo Rides

As we began to push, Alfredo yelled out a congratulations for getting the room, then chided us for pushing up the hill. I jokingly offered him my bike. He laughed then swung his leg over the seat and accepted the challenge. He huffed and puffed all the way to the top, while his pals yelled praise and encouragement.

WOW, CNN in English. Our room had three beds. As we pulled the bikes inside I noticed a squished frog on the door frame. Alfredo said, "Poor frog. Will you get toilet paper, por favor?" He removed it, as we all felt badly for the loss. Life there was tough, even for frogs.

Cold showers? Hard to believe at that high room rate. I called and the desk said they'd send someone. After a thirty minute wait we waded into the chill.

A glass of wine helped warm the cockles as we shivered dry and watched CNN. We took our bottle of wine along for dinner and it was a good thing. They did have white wine but at $20 per bottle. They allowed ours, even opened and iced it. We were seated in the entry area. The main dining room was full of Brits and Germans. The place was a tourist stop. A resorts of sorts.

Chris and Eileen

Two of the English tourists, Chris and Eileen, asked us to sit in the main room with them. What a joy to chat, in English. He was in sales and marketing but had recently downsized his career. Now teaching, he earned less money but was enjoying it a great deal

 more. Eileen also worked three days a week. The four of us enjoyed a pretty good buffet. We made several trips.

Back at room 415 we found a large frog had taken up residence. I chased him for a while then lost him under the furniture. A Larry King Live re-run kept us awake for about twenty minutes.

As Cat lay relaxing, a frog hopped onto the bed.

Memories of toxic frogs in Central America danced in her head. The frog was filled with greater fear than Cat. He took off in large hops ending up near the door. Our effort to chase him out failed. He leapt under the dresser. Then a mom-sized jumper climbed  the wall and squeezed into a crack near the ceiling. To complete the invasion, a cute little baby came hopping across the floor. We had been invaded by an entire family. It made getting up and getting going easy for Cat.

The included buffet breakfast was the best we'd had in Cuba. Eggs, bacon, and fresh fruit. Rate had its privileges. We sat and ate as we enjoyed watching and listening to tourists compare notes in their British and German accents. We paid the bill on the way out and promised to leave the key with the chambermaid.

Bikes loaded, we looked but failed to find the maid. Coasting down the drive that Alfredo had peddled up, was a cinch. My legs were stiff as I walked up the steep walkway to return the key. Inside, I met Chris and Eileen and bid them goodbye. As I tried in vain to buy a bottle of water, Chris insisted on giving us theirs. He rushed off to their room to get it, then met us on the street below. He said, "I'm a club cyclist, I know the amount of water required to pedal long distances."

Sancti Spiritus to Santa Clara, 103 Ks
A Missed Turn Added 16 Ks on a Rainy Day

It was an ups and downs ride on a narrow road for 27 Ks, back to the Autopista. At lunch, we got the last two sandwiches they had at a roadside restaurant. Two nice young guys worked hard to serve us then helped get the bikes inside as it started to pour rain. We ate slowly hoping for a break in the weather. When it dwindled to a drizzle we pushed off as the boys cheered while waving goodbye. Within just a few minutes we were in a wind-driven downpour; the remnants of the hurricane's passing as she trailed off toward Florida.

Passing this billboard reminded us that as on TV, the only advertising seen anywhere was all about the revolution and the brave followers of Castro who ended the brutal dictatorship of Fulgencio Batista.

Batista had aligned himself with the wealthiest Cuban landowners. Those who owned the largest sugar plantations. He presided over a stagnating economy that widened the gap between rich and poor Cubans. Eventually it reached the point where most of the sugar industry was in U.S. hands, and foreigners owned 70% of the arable land. As such, Batista's increasingly corrupt and repressive government then began to systematically profit from the exploitation of Cuba's commercial interests, by negotiating lucrative relationships with both the American mafia, who controlled the drug, gambling, and prostitution businesses in Havana, and with large U.S.-based multinational companies who were awarded lucrative contracts. It is estimated that as many as 20,000 were imprisoned or executed during Batista's reign. However, many feel that Castro eventually became the NEW dictator.

We peddled onward past kilometer marker 247 where I'd estimated we would find Santa Clara. It was pouring rain and the wind was blowing hard, pushing us along. At marker 254 we talked with a couple of guys getting ready to go fishing in a rushing river. They pointed back and said, "Diez kilometers." We'd missed the turn, overshot it by 10 Ks.

Back to a little bar in the center divider. Hopeful to hook a ride, we talked with people there. Even offered to pay a guy with a roof rack on his Lada to take us back to town. He declined. After a failed attempt at calling he suggested trying the service station further back. Cycling against the torrents of wind-driven rain was brutal.

The people at the station were less than helpful. We split a pizza, weighed our options, then decided to ride. Another 2 Ks to the turn off for the Autopista to the left, left us facing the full force of the wind. Cat's front shifter wasn't dropping into low gear. That was a constant problem when her hands were wet. We had to walk up one hill. As we pushed, a young guy ran out then walked along with us shivering and asking for a T-shirt or a pen.

A hard-fought 10 Ks back into town only to get lost. The best news after an entire day in it, the rain stopped. Asking and asking we finally found signs for Hotel Santa Clara Libre, the hotel that

Alfredo had recommended. Through narrow city streets in a mist we at last cycled up to the hotel at 5:30 pm.

Soaked and quivering, we checked in. They made us leave the bikes in a locked, air-conditioned room with their computer system. Our ears and fingers froze as we removed the necessary bags with clothing and computer from the refrigerated room.

Our room was on the fifth floor. Two pieces of good news: the wonderful old elevator worked, even had an elevator operator wearing white gloves. The second was even better than the elevator news: HOT WATER!

Warm showers then off to dinner upstairs on floor 10. Red Cuban wine with good food but portions small. Once again, the prices again were surprisingly gigantic.

Hector played song after song on his upright piano. We sang along to his delight as he played a medley of Steven Foster tunes. When he moved on to big band show tunes we continued to sing and even danced.

Our request that they program CNN in English fell on deaf ears. Cat watched a little Spanish language TV. I went to sleep as soon as my head hit the pillow.

The Sights of Santa Clara

79

The included breakfast was so small it was hardly worth the wait for the elevator and the extremely slow service. A young couple from Seattle came in. They too, must have been there visiting without official sanction. They were very nervous about talking with us. They sat down, waited, asked a couple of questions, then left. They were told they couldn't order eggs. There was no selection available other than tiny ham and cheese sandwiches supplemented with a box of pear juice and a cup of coffee. We ordered a couple more sandwiches to quell the hunger pangs knotting our stomachs.

Off to the bank. They would change pesos to kooks after we sat and waited. I wanted a picture of the picture hanging on their wall, Fidel with an AK47 held on high. The guard quickly moved to me and motioned no pictures. I questioned, even sort of argued, but he was adamant and he was the one with the gun. We had slipped the suspect 1995 - 500 peso bill into our stack. This bank didn't seem to have a problem or missed it, as they counted and re-counted.

We delivered our sweaty clothing to the chambermaid. Don't you hate that name, chambermaid? Sounds very subservient and un-socialistic. She promised to have them washed and dried before she left for home.

We ran in to the young Seattle couple again. They had found a Casa Particular and the woman there cooked them a good breakfast. For us it was another pizza luncheon. We also found an inexpensive white wine and bottled water.

We took a taxi to see the famous revolutionary sights of Santa Clara. First stop, a huge square filled with a unique pattern of pavers and statue of Che holding his trusty AK 47. A proper memorial for a proper hero.

Next stop, the famous statue of Che holding a child in his arms. It is revered because it was said that as Che and his revolutionaries swept into town, they frightened the young girl who began to cry. Che took her up in his arms to console her.

Che, a Compassionate Man

Many people visit this site to leave flowers to honor Che and the child. Finally a visit to the site where Che and his cadre of 80 revolutionaries derailed a troop and ammo train defeating 408 Batista government troops. A simple but very effective plan, Che had a farmer plow up the train track ahead of the train then, when it stopped, they plowed the track up behind and trapped it. It was sounding more and more to us as though the Batista guys weren't very motivated. Or, was it that to the victors, go the spoils of history? Our driver explained that, though many of the Batista troops ran, more than half joined Che and the revolution.

The Beginning of The End For Batista

Santa Clara, Cuba's third largest city and the capital of Las Villas Province, was attacked December 29, 1958, by Ernesto Che Guevara. His volunteers were outnumbered ten to one by Cuban army forces. Che's cadres were aided by many locals who hampered the movement of the army's tanks and armored vehicles by blocking the streets with parked cars.

Che felt that the capture of the armored train had to be a priority. He mobilized tractors from the local university and pulled up the rails, derailing the train. The officers on the train asked for a truce. The enlisted soldiers were demoralized. Some began talking with Che's rebels. They were tired of fighting against their own people. Within a short time Che's troops took control and many Cuban army soldiers deserted to join the rebels.

The train was loaded with weapons that fell to the rebels. The capture of the train proved to be a key tipping point in the revolution. Despite the next day's newspapers in Havana arrogantly claiming a Batista victory at Santa Clara, radio broadcasts from Castro's revolutionaries hastened the surrender of the Cuban army. The reports also spread news that Castro's rebels were surging toward Havana to take over the government.

La Provencia Granma

You can never get too much Granma! The day before, we had cycled from Provencia Santiago de Cuba into Provencia Granma, formerly known as Provencia Oriente.

In August 1958, Castro's forces opened four battlefronts against the Batista army. On November 20 Fidel led his troops to a victory in the town Guisa, 20 Ks southeast of Bayamo. In December, three columns under the command of Che Guevara, Camilo Cienfuegos, and Jaime Vega proceeded westward toward the provincial capital of Santa Clara.

Vega's column was ambushed and destroyed. The surviving two columns reached the central provinces where they joined efforts with several other resistance groups not under the command of Castro. Cienfuegos was victorious in the Battle of Yaguajay on December 30, 1958 (earning him the nickname "The Hero of Yaguajay"). The next day, in a scene of great confusion, the city of Santa Clara was captured by the forces of Che Guevara. News of these defeats caused Batista to panic. He fled Cuba for the Dominican Republic.

Castro's advance on Havana was extensively photographed by US photographer Burt Glinn

Rebels arriving in Havana, January 1959

A Sleep Over in Santa Clara

Tired of the high prices for eating out, we found cheeseburgers

85

at a cafeteria. They were unbelievably inexpensive, like all things paid for in Cuban pesos. Fifty pesos (about $2.00) for both. Delicious and super-sized, too. Taking them to go we enjoyed fabulous-tasting burgers and an HBO movie in English back in our room. That was until someone below flipped a switch and we lost the finale of the film. The movie channel was replaced by an all-Spanish Cuban political show. So it was early to bed.

Santa Clara to Colon, 112Ks
The Case of the Disappearing Laundry

A bit of panic set in as our laundry hadn't made it back. A call to the front desk brought reassurances, so we went up in the classic elevator to breakfast. Same tiny sandwiches, same little box of pear juice, and same cup of weak, uninspiring coffee.

Back in the room our clothing was still on the missing list. We decided to pack as best we could and take the bags down to the bikes. As we emerged from the elevator, our clothing came to us in a stranger's hands. No sign of our friendly laundry lady. They wanted more than the two kooks she'd quoted. We stood our ground as they were late getting them back to us.

Cat ran next door and bought two large sandwiches for less than one-quarter of the price for those upstairs. We bagged them as backup, just in case we couldn't find food on the road. A late start but we were finally out the door by 9:30 am.

Jose, On His Way to Havana/Heaven

It was an ask - ask kind of morning working our way out of town. We had to backtrack all the way to the highway. Along the way we met Jose. Wrapped in a burlap skirt, he was on a religious journey. His little wagon was covered with verses from the bible. We tried to chat but fell short on language skills. He got the point across that he too was going to Havana. However his journey would keep him shuffling until at least Christmas. That was dedication to his greater power. As great, maybe greater than our dedication to complete this crazy bike ride through Cuba and ultimately back to

California. Cat shuddered at the thought. She was really beginning to dream about the easy life back in Mexico.

El Camino National, The Bumpy Road

Off and on again rain kept things cooler as we rode through green countryside covered with rice fields. We'd left the Autopista and were cycling the Camino National, the old road. One fellow we talked with called it the bumpy road, and it was. A lot of the pavement was either broken up or had been covered with a new layer of asphalt and they'd forgotten to iron out the bumps.

We saw a couple of little stores but pueblos were few and far between. We decided to enjoy the sandwiches and drinks we had on board. We found a shady spot and ate as the rest of the Cuban world, what little there was of it out there, continued to roll by.

Later, at a stop for soft drinks, a guy named Tomas came walking around the building and was shocked to meet us. He asked where we were going. When we told him in our halting Spanish, "Todo el mundo," he said, "Oh my god!" A couple others stood listening as we struggled with language. I took their picture. One wore an Ohio State University shirt, the other had a cap with "Miami Heat" emblazoned upon it.

The Little Town Called George Washington

Riding past a cerveceria (brewery/pub) the guys all called out inviting us in for a beer. Sorry amigos, just a little too early for drinking. Then a strange sight: a little old steam engine named George Washington and a monument to our first president. Can you believe the little village, home of the little train, was named George Washington?

The best info we found was that during the American Revolutionary War, "The Havana Ladies," a group of Cuban mothers, heard General Washington's plea for desperately needed funds and raised an astonishing amount for that time. They sent to Virginia the equivalent in today's money of $28 million. This has received little exposure in American history books, but is well documented. The inscription that the "Ladies of Havana" wrote on their contribution was: "So the American mothers' sons are not born as slaves."

Otto and Lazaro Find an X Rated Room

We rode into the service station in Colon at 5:00 and asked about a hotel. Otto, the attendant, pointed across the street and said, "I think ees fully book. Estudiantes aqui for ceety (city) meeting." He ran across checked and returned with the bad news.

What about a Casa Particular? They asked around, then told us there were none in town. We were really getting concerned when Otto told us to relax, that they would help find a place. He whistled and a young boy, Lazaro, on a small bike wheeled in. He listened, then set off on a quest to find a room. We got beers and sat on the ground near the bikes. One beer, no word from Lazaro. Two beers, still no word. We began to worry, we needed a shower, not more beer.

A couple of other hombres came over and asked if we needed a place to stay. They'd been drinking. Otto signaled for us to disregard them. We just shook our heads, "No." It almost felt like they were all testing us. At last Lazaro came wheeling in with good news. He'd found a place but we had to wait until after 6:30. Darkness, we assumed. Obviously, this was another unlicensed Casa. We could care less but understood the reason. Sitting on the ground and sweating wasn't comfortable or comforting. As dusk approached, Otto shook our hands and waved for us to follow Lazaro.

Renier, Lazara, and Andrea

About six blocks off the highway we rode up to the gate of a nice-looking house. A guy threw the gate open and urged us to enter quickly. Renier took us to the back side of their garage. It had been converted into a complete apartment. The bed was large and comfortable. They had a tape player with romantic music. Even a mirror appropriately placed on the ceiling. Yikes! An illegal Casa Particular sex hotel! Entrepreneurial spirit: find a need, then fill the need. Basic capitalism! There was a refrigerator full of beers. Pressure off, I enjoyed a third cool one.

Renier and his girlfriend Lazara, told us they had no food for dinner but we could use their kitchen. After very refreshing showers we went to the house where Andrea, Renier's mom, helped us with pots, pans, and dishes.

We had a very good meal home-cooked by Cat and served at the family's dining table. Pasta with a can of tuna.

By 9:00 pm we'd cleared the table. Weary, we fell directly into the soft bed and stared at ourselves in the mirror as we fell to sleep.

Colon to Matanzas, 89 Ks

A knock on the door at 7:00 am. They really wanted us out early to avoid problems. By the way, usually anything before 9:00 am was early in Cuba. We pushed the bikes around the garage, shook hands with Renier and Andrea, then slipped out the gate. Pedaling away, we hoped we'd gone un-noticed by nosey neighbors.

There were no restaurants open. Not even the service station where we'd sat drinking the beers. The sign there said, "Abierto 24 Horas," but that just wasn't so. Otto wasn't there but a stranger had no idea where we might find food.

Cat saw a line at a stall for fresh bread on the other side of the street. We pushed across and she fell into the queue. That caused a stir. A gal came out and in English said, "This bakery is for local people only." She spun around, went back inside and immediately returned with four fresh-baked rolls. She handed them to us and refused payment, then wished us well. Others in the line smiled and nodded approval. Remembering our search for lunch a week earlier when Mary, Milda, and one-armed Juan had treated us. We decided those very low-cost stores and bakeries were specifically for the hard-working, low-paid locals.

Brain Surgeons Earn $20, Teachers $10

Three blocks down the street, we saw what looked like a bar. Upon closer observation we saw people carrying out ham sandwiches. We ordered, fearing that might be the only food in town. As we ate, a fellow walked up and spoke to us in good English. Miguel was a high school math teacher. He said, "I don't like how the system works here in Cuba. I teach math and languages and I'm paid the same as all other teachers, 250 pesos per month." Then he did the math for us, "That is ten U.S. dollars, these shoes I wear cost twenty dollars. Imagine, I work two months just to buy shoes." He added, "I could make better living in Havana, but cost of living is much more, and I would have to get government approval to make the move." We suggested that stores for the people with inexpensive basic food, as well as rents and utilities, were government subsidized.

However, his anger was directed toward the new CUC stores. "First you have to change pesos to kooks, which costs money," he said. "Then you find prices in these stores are so much higher than wages, that a family can't even afford to buy a toy for their child."

We had seen the way people stood, faces pressed against the windows of the CUC stores, looking longingly at the untouchable or at least unaffordable items inside. His shoes were expensive looking, probably purchased at the CUC store. So, thanks to the teacher earning half as much as a brain surgeon, we'd just had a glimpse inside a society reliant on government subsidy.

More on-and-off-again rain as we rode through lush farmland. Then at Limonar, a pueblo off the highway, we took a turn onto small dirt streets looking for food. It wasn't easy getting through the dusty streets and into town.

Cat spotted a lady carrying a pizza. She pointed and told us that there was a house, a casa, where they make them. It was just that, a house. The industrious family was working hard cooking pizza. Hungry people like us were lining up. We sat in the shade across the street as we ate the tasty morsels. The pizzas attracted more than people. The street was also abuzz with a cloud of hungry flies. We used a lot of energy waving and swatting trying to keep them off our pizzas.

As we shooed the flies, we noticed several people eating soft ice cream cones. Ah, dessert! The government was providing cheap dessert too: cones just five cents each. The guy dispensing was fun to watch and listen to, as well. He laughed and joked with his customers. Many were kids from the adjacent school.

I wanted a picture of all the kids but when I pulled out the camera, a woman, their teacher, put up a hand and said, "No photo." Another missed opportunity for some great shots, due to authoritarian rules.

The road into Matanzas had its ups and downs. We pedaled hard up then crossed a bridge into heavy traffic only to learn, after asking, that we had passed the street to the main plaza. Back up and over, then more up into town. Our guidebook suggested there were two hotels. One, it said, was under re-construction. As we found the one the book advised, a classic built before the turn of the twentieth century, a couple of guys found us. They seemed to be fighting a war of words with each other as they tried to get us to follow them. Each was touting a different Casa Particular. Both were saying that neither hotel was open. Disbelieving, I went inside and as they'd said the restaurant was open but the hotel was closed for repairs. The waiter also confirmed that the only other hotel was also closed.

So we were at the mercy of the two jerks. One began stressing the fact that he was a taxi driver. He didn't want money: he would take us to a nice Casa that sends him customers. He won the battle but as we walked away, the other guy muttered something about "Ladron" (thief) and warned us to be careful.

Our new guide, Elio, continued to insist he only wanted to promote more business for his taxi. When I asked where his taxi was he said, "At home." The more we were around him, the less we liked him. He kept up a running patter but didn't listen. At the door of the Casa he said, "This house belongs to my friends." A woman answered the bell and told us that she was fully booked. Elio's credibility dropped another notch. We began to think that his gimmick was to ask the Casa owners for money.

The woman spoke with him in Spanish. We got some of the conversation. She had friends who had a room. I actually asked Elio to shut up a couple of times as she spoke. She insisted on writing the names and address of her friends. Elio kept claiming he didn't need it. I insisted that we wanted it. I even blatantly questioned whether she knew Elio. She didn't. Then she yelled, and another woman came to the door. She told us in Spanglish that this woman would take us to the friend's place. Elio knew he'd been outed.

Isidro and Noelia

We pushed and followed as Elio chattered with the woman. Casa operators Isidro and Noelia, greeted us at their door. They thanked the woman and dismissed Elio. We think he was trying to tell them he had brought us to them. Isidro just waved him off. We thanked Elio and were delighted to see him go. Isidro commented about Elio. He said, "No honest, negre," as he touched the light skin on his own arm. Elio was black, Cubano pero negre. So perhaps all was not rainbows and lollipops between brothers of different colors in Cuba's socialist society.

The house was wonderful, as wonderful, as Isidro and Noelia.

The room they had for us was downstairs, separated from the house. A nice bedroom with private bath. Usually, they had warm water however, the power was out, thus their suicide shower wouldn't work. Isidro had us put the bikes in his little garage adjacent to our room. Then we just sat resting and relaxing while waiting for electricity. I made a tour of the house and took pictures.

Noelia told us they were in their mid-seventies and had been married for fifty-five years. They had lived in the house for eleven years and operated the Casa for just the past two.

Tired of waiting, we walked to a store. Isidro had pointed at a bodega and said, "Si, vino!". It didn't have wine but the clerk sent us to another that did. Back at our wonderful new home, we found that the power was still out. So, cold showers.

Dinner by candle and headlights. Noelia made a fantastic meal

of meat and vegetables for an additional six kooks. (The room cost fifteen). Then as we ate, she meticulously filled out the paperwork for room rental including our passport numbers. We were pretty sure now that meals are a tax-free bonus for the Casa operators.

A Letter to San Pedro, California

Noelia told us they had a nephew living in San Pedro, California. She was very excited to hear that we would cycle close to his home in a few months. So excited, in fact, that she wrote a letter and asked if we'd deliver it. Of course we would.

Another windfall profit for Isidro and Noelia and a wonderful breakfast for us. She cooked eggs and banana strips, fried like bacon served with toast and blended guava juice. They both stood worrying as we pushed through the house and lifted the bikes over the courtyard door jamb. What wonderful people, the kind you feel you've known all your life. A handshake for Isidro and kiss on the cheek for Noelia. Cat got kisses and good wishes from both.

Chapter 8: The Bay of Pigs and Russian Missiles

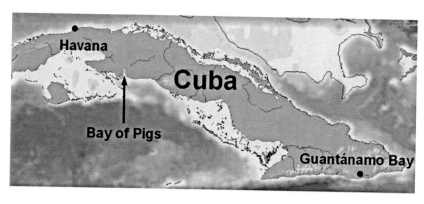

Somewhere off to the south, maybe 30 miles, there lies a famous/infamous little spear-pointed bay called Bahía de Cochinos, The Bay of Pigs. Why Pigs? Best Answer: The English translation of cochinos as "pigs" might be erroneous, as in all probability here it refers to a species of triggerfish (Balistes vetula), rather than pigs.

Almost as soon as he came to power, Castro nationalized American-dominated industries such as sugar and mining, introduced land reform schemes, and called on other Latin American governments to act with more autonomy. In response, early in 1960 President Eisenhower became very concerned at the direction Castro's government was taking. He allocated $13.1 million to the CIA to plan Castro's overthrow. The CIA was to recruit 1,400 Cuban exiles living in Miami and begin training them to overthrow Castro. Eisenhower's extensive military background left him skeptical of the plan. He decided to pass it on to the new Kennedy administration.

In January 1961, just days after his inauguration, President Kennedy severed diplomatic relations with Cuba and stepped up preparations for an invasion. Some State Department and other advisers to JFK maintained that Castro posed no real threat to America, but the new president believed that organizing the Cuban leader's removal would show Russia, China, and skeptical Americans, that he was serious about winning the Cold War.

97

Kennedy had inherited Eisenhower's CIA campaign to train and equip a guerilla army of Cuban exiles, but he had some doubts about the wisdom of the plan. He didn't want "direct, overt" intervention by the American military in Cuba: The Soviets would likely see this as an act of war and might retaliate. However, CIA officers told him they could keep U.S. involvement in the invasion a secret and, if all went according to plan, the campaign would spark an anti-Castro uprising on the island.

The first part of the plan was to destroy Castro's tiny air force, making it impossible for his military to resist the invaders. On April 15, 1961, a group of Cuban exiles took off from Nicaragua in a squadron of American B-26 bombers, painted to look like stolen Cuban planes, and conducted a strike against Cuban airfields. It turned out that Castro and his advisers knew about the raid and had moved the planes. Frustrated, Kennedy began to suspect that the plan the CIA had promised would be "both clandestine and successful" might in fact be "too large to be clandestine and too small to be successful."

Beginning in January of 1960, CIA planes from Florida, some with American pilots, raided Cuban fields with napalm-type bombs to burn sugar cane, as part of an attempt to bring about the overthrow of the Castro government.

It was too late to apply the brakes. On April 17, the Cuban exile brigade began its invasion at an isolated spot on the island's southern shore known as the Bay of Pigs. Almost immediately, the invasion was a disaster. The CIA had wanted to keep it a secret for as long as possible, but a radio station on the beach broadcast every detail of the operation to listeners across Cuba. Unexpected coral reefs sank some of the exiles' ships as they pulled into shore. Backup paratroopers landed in the wrong place. Before long, Castro's troops had pinned the invaders on the beach, and the exiles surrendered after less than a day of fighting; 114 were killed and more than 1,100 were taken prisoner.

According to many historians, the CIA and the Cuban exile brigade believed that President Kennedy would eventually allow the American military to intervene in Cuba on their behalf. However, the president was resolute: As much as he did not want to "abandon Cuba to the communists," he said, he would not start a fight that might end in World War III.

In response to the failed Bay of Pigs invasion of 1961, and the presence of American Jupiter ballistic missiles in Italy and Turkey, Soviet leader Nikita Khrushchev decided to agree to Cuba's request to place nuclear missiles on the island to deter future invasions. An agreement was reached during a secret meeting between Khrushchev and Castro in July 1962, and construction of a number of missile launch facilities started later that summer.

The 1962 midterm elections were under way in the United States and the White House had denied charges that it was ignoring

dangerous Soviet missiles ninety miles from Florida. These missile preparations were confirmed when an Air Force U-2 spy plane produced clear photographic evidence of medium-range (SS-4) and intermediate-range (R-14) ballistic missile facilities. The United States established a military blockade to prevent further missiles from reaching Cuba. It announced that they would not permit offensive weapons to be delivered to Cuba and demanded that the weapons already in Cuba be dismantled and returned to the USSR.

After a long period of tense negotiations, an agreement was reached between U.S. President John F. Kennedy and Khrushchev. Kennedy purportedly said, "We were eye to eye and the other fellow blinked!" Publicly, the Soviets would dismantle their offensive weapons in Cuba and return them to the Soviet Union, subject to United Nations verification, in exchange for a U.S. public declaration and agreement never to invade Cuba again without direct provocation. Secretly, the United States also agreed that it would dismantle all U.S.-built Jupiter MRBMs, which, unknown to the public, had been deployed in Turkey and Italy against the Soviet Union.

When all offensive missiles and Ilyushin Il-28 light bombers had been withdrawn from Cuba, the blockade was formally ended on November 20, 1962. The negotiations between the United States

and the Soviet Union highlighted the necessity of a quick, clear, and direct communication line between Washington and Moscow. Proving that some good comes from all things, the "Red Phone" was installed in both cities.

The State Department Policy Planning Staff, proposed direct communication links between Moscow and Washington. Objections from others in the State Department, the U.S. military, and the Kremlin delayed introduction.

The 1962 Cuban Missile Crisis made the hotline a priority. During the standoff, official diplomatic messages typically took six hours to deliver; unofficial channels, such as via television network correspondents, had to be used, too, as they were quicker.

The "hotline", as it would come to be known, was established after the signing of a "Memorandum of Understanding" by representatives of the Soviet Union and the United States.

In January 1898, the USS Maine was dispatched to Cuba, to protect U.S. interests. At that time, more than 8,000 U.S. citizens resided in the country. On February 15, 1898, the Maine exploded and sank in Havana harbor. It became a major rallying call for the Spanish–American War, (Remember the Maine!) and caused the U.S. to finally intercede on Cuba's behalf.

On March 4, 1960, the French freighter La Coubre, carrying 76 tons of Belgian munitions exploded, killing 100. The cause of the blast, is often attributed to the CIA, attempting to overthrow the government of Fidel Castro.

Chapter 9: Elian, Cuban Five, Fidel in Our Havana Hotel

Imelda and Hilary from Ireland

Back up and over the bridge, around a corner, then in to more up. Long slow pulls into steep rolling hills. Moving slowly, we were cooled by wind and drizzle. Then as the dark clouds parted, we ran headlong into a couple of gals on bikes. Hilary and Imelda were from Ireland. One from Northern Ireland and the other from the Republic of Ireland. They both lived and worked in Dublin. They were on their first day of a two-week cycling adventure. A sort of resort to resort trip. Later, they were going to fly to the island of Trinidad and complete their adventure.

Imelda was having trouble shifting gears. I checked and found that her rear derailleur was loose. A twist of the allen wrench, and problem solved. Her seat was loose, not a good thing riding on a loose caboose. Ever wonder why the citizens of most other open, free countries travel in Cuba?

Coastal at Last – Eloy, and Nintendo

Once on the downhill run, we coasted all the way to the coast. Hungry, we pulled into Pueblo Santa Cruz del Norte. Asking for pizza we found a cafeteria that looked pretty bad. The guy there shook his head regarding pizza, then pointed to a house next door. We pushed there and a guy on the sidewalk agreed, then called out. A woman came to the door and somehow got the point across that she wasn't cooking pizza that afternoon. As we turned to go back to the dingy cafeteria, she said, "I make something for you." Claudina became our hostess with the mostess. She invited us inside and allowed us to park the bikes inside her fenced yard.

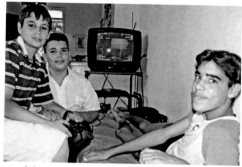

She seated us on wooden rocking chairs near her fourteen-year-old son, Eloy. He was lying down on a mattress on the floor, playing a Nintendo wrestling game. One of his friends was playing against him, another stood watching. For us it was like seeing our grandkids. Then as Claudina brought eggs and bread, out she said, "I make for you omelete." Then she told us, "Eloy haves livers infections. Eet ees very serious he must lay down and rest. Our relative een the U.S. hear of this and send Nintendo game for him."

A really great gift for a sick boy. Especially when the boy lived in Cuba. It was impossible to buy this kind of video game in Cuba even if you had the money. Claudina asked, "Ees thees game expensive?" We guessed it would cost at least $150 U.S. That made her smile, perhaps knowing that her relatives cared that much for her and her son.

Shawnee, Oklahoma?

Another surprise: after she served a wonderful omelet with cheese and lots of bread, she brought out an envelope for us to see. It was from relatives of her father. The amazing thing was, they live in Shawnee, Oklahoma, the little town where my mother had been born. It strained our Spanish but we think we got that across to her. After all that and with full stomachs, we paid the one kook she'd asked, then slipped another into her hand. We wondered whether, one kook was her regular price or had she made a deal for two interesting foreigners. She did okay when the exchange rate, kook to peso, was factored in.

Back at it, we still had 50 Ks to cycle into Havana. The ride was fairly flat along the coast and through one of Cuba's small oil-producing areas. There were wells pumping right out on the sandy

beach. It felt a lot like Southern California. We were betting that if Cuba discovered substantial oil, the USA would cancel that damned embargo immediately. A good day's business cures all ills!

Cat Gets Strip Searched

A stop for soft drinks at a big traffic circle in big traffic and we learned we had to cross the Bay of Havana on a ferry. There was a tunnel under the bay but bicycles weren't allowed. Then it was ask, ask, ask, until a young girl said, "Turn here, go straight to water." It was farther than we'd thought and tough riding in rush-hour traffic. It was 5:30 by the time we arrived at the ferry.

The crowd of people were pressing against a chain-link fence trying to get aboard and get home. The guard motioned for us to

push the bikes and follow a woman with a baby carriage. Inside the gate, another, more surly policeman demanded that I open my bags. I argued a bit, then obeyed, by opening the one on my handlebars. He poked around, then asked what else we had. I told him clothing and camping equipment. He waved me through. Cat followed the baby carriage lady. Her police person was a big, gruff-looking woman. She commanded Cat to remove and open all her panniers. When I complained, my formerly surly, now friendly fellow told her that he was satisfied. She let him know she wasn't and insisted that Cat empty *all* her bags.

So we began taking her bags off and stacking them on the table. I made sure we moved slowly, holding up all the others in line. They were trying to push past. We stood our ground as we took the bags off Cat's bike. The woman, true to her word, had us open every bag and empty them. We continued to move slowly, jamming things back in the bags that she'd pawed through and placing them back onto the bike racks. Cat was a bit embarrassed but my strategy was that the boat wouldn't leave us if there were still others behind us.

Good strategy: we did get on board just as they pulled up the gangway. Note, the nasty guard woman only made Cat strip the bags off the bikes, not the clothing off her backside.

On board we met Stefan from Germany, who was traveling along with Enda and Eion from Ireland. They'd met at a hostel and Stefan found moving around in threes preferable to being a loner. At the dock in Havana, the guys helped Cat lift her bike ashore.

Thank goodness for the map of Havana Wilber had sold us before we left, and for Isidro and Noelia, who'd called a family friend and arranged a Casa Particular. We cycled along the waterfront and onto the world famous Havana Malecon. The damage from the hurricane was obvious. Parts of the Malecon wall were gone, collapsed into the sea. Several places on the street had recently been repaired and repaved.

The sun was setting as we rolled up to the Hotel Cohiba, our meeting place with Marvin, the son of the Casa Particular operator.

A caravan of classics surrounded us. The famous old cars of Cuba were picking up French hotel guests for a cruise around town on their way to dinner. Tourist groups, curious about the old cars, were keeping the classic car owners busy.

I felt a little out of place entering the opulent Cohiba lobby. Sweaty and more than likely smelly, I asked the concierge for a telephone. He looked me up and down, then pointed to the communication center. They had phones and computers available. The woman in charge, directed me to a row of telephones. I dialed and Marvin answered. He asked that we wait while he walked to meet us. "Don't worry," he said. "We are very close."

It took ten minutes for Marvin to get there, then after hellos he led us out into the darkness. They must have been running generators, at the Cohiba. All the adjacent neighborhoods were as black as pitch. The walk was a struggle in the dark. Headlights from the passing cars momentarily blinded us. The real struggle came at Marvin's house. It was actually an apartment on the second floor. Fortunately, Marvin grabbed the back of each bike and once he understood not to lift, just push, we moved them up quickly. Boy were we tired, completely sapped of energy.

We pulled our headlights out of the bag while searching for food and wondered why we hadn't thought of that as we were walking and pushing.

Cat began cooking rice and canned meat from our bags, on their gas stove. Marvin and I went to a local cafeteria to buy beers.

We decided to eat while waiting for the return of the electricity to heat the bath water. Another dining experience by bicycle headlights.

Marvin's mom, Chela, told us (with his help translating) how deep the water had been during the hurricane. Also how afraid she had been during the howling wind and darkness. Their flat was located just a half block from the Malecon. The storm surge had flooded the area to a depth of eight feet. It came up the stairs but didn't get inside their apartment. She worried about her beautiful furniture. Cat could relate to Chela's hurricane fears.

All conversation ended when Marvin left for the evening with his girlfriend. There were others there, but none spoke English.

Our wait for electricity and the return of warm water ended in fatigue. It was cold showers, then a warm bed.

A Walk Around Havana

The power had returned by morning. We had lights but the water was still cold. Marvin was up early and dressed fit to kill. He was headed to a commercial show that we'd seen advertised on posters, all over Cuba. He was really excited about the possibilities for a young guy. He had told us, "I am so very happy that you are here. You give me a chance to practice my English." He went on, "I'm twenty-eight years old and still a student. My idea now is to

107

find work in tourism, hopefully at a hotel where I would make tips as well as wages." Our bet was that those who dole out such jobs would be requiring kickbacks. We didn't ask — no reason to burst his bubble.

Some Want Change, Some Fear Change!

Marvin took time to talk a bit about his family. "My father died from a stroke, eight years ago. My mother, Chela, is a breast cancer survivor. She had partial mastectomy two years ago. I want to go to USA or I want to see things change in Cuba. I want to make big money." Chela spoke and Marvin said, "My madre think, if she leave Cuba or things change, she would be at risk, without health insurance. I have been think of go to Mexico, to find a woman to marry. Many young Cuban guys do that, to get to USA." Those

were exactly the same feelings I'd heard expressed in the Soviet Union, in 1989. Older comrades who had worked all their lives in and for the system felt they'd earned government support for their golden years. The ambitious young wanted change instantly, one way or the other. When we thought about it, their feelings were the same as those of older people in the USA, like me, who receive Social Security.

Marvin left and again, all conversation stopped. Chela plopped down in front of the television.

Daniel, was Marvin's brother. He lived with their grandmother. He was there visiting. Assef, a Syrian, was in Cuba studying to be a pharmacist. He and his girlfriend were renting a room from Chela.

Neither spoke English. They seemed embarrassed to even try.

The following day was spent walking to the Havana Libre Hotel, and back. We met with Wilber and apologized for forgetting to bring back his Lonely Planet guide book promising to return it the next day. We also confirmed with the front desk that we could bring the bikes over the next morning and leave them with the bellmen. A first step in making our move from Chela's Casa Particular to the luxury of the Havana Libre. The walk back was a photo shoot of Cuba's wonderful old American classic cars.

Wilber called a friend at Cubano Air and got the exact amount of the departure tax and the per-kilo cost for our overweight luggage. We had been scraping by, not spending a penny more than we had to. Poverty wasn't a lifestyle we were accustomed to. The figures Wilber received left us with only thirteen kooks per day disposable cash. As the old saying goes, poverty sucks.

Wilber was off work the next day. He gave us his home address and invited us to stop by to meet his wife and new baby boy.

He apologized in advance for the condition of their home. He lived near Chela's place in a first floor flat. The water had been up to his chest before it finally subsided. The greatest loss of all was

109

toilet paper. All toilet paper in the stores had been ruined by the flood waters. Guess we could say, "It was *wiped out*."

The forces of Guevara and Cienfuegos entered Havana at about the same time. They had met no opposition from Santa Clara to the capital city. Fidel Castro arrived later after a long victory march.

Fidel and his Revolutionaries in Our Hotel

Emily From Vancouver, BC

There was a display of photos, in the lobby of the Hotel Libre. One showed Fidel and his comrades, taken there in 1959. Like a conquering horde, they had flooded in to the lobby, of what was the Hilton Hotel, at that time. Castro and his boys commandeered the seventeenth floor. It became their revolutionary headquarters.

The Libre, also had a display of photos decrying the incarceration and mistreatment of "The Cuban Five."

As we read the posters on the hotel wall, Emily asked if we were cycling the world. She'd noticed the maps on our shirts, our strange suntans, and put two and two together. She too was a cyclist, not there or then, but she had cycled from her hometown Vancouver, BC, Canada, to Panama a couple of years earlier. She'd come to Cuba to study Spanish. Though her class had been cancelled, her professor was tutoring her privately. Immersion is the best way to learn the language, culture, and customs of local folks. Emily, like all our Canadians neighbors to the north, traveled freely in Cuba.

Remember the Cuban Five?

The Cuban Five? Five Cuban guys that had attempted to liberate Elian Gonzales from the clutches of his uncle in Miami.

You remember the story. His mother took him for a boat ride to Florida. The boat went under and she died. Elian survived and made it ashore in Florida. His uncle's family held him during the international fight over who should be awarded his custody. We didn't remember the story of these five guys but did remember that the U.S. Attorney General, Janet Reno, finally decided that

under U.S. law, the father would prevail in these kinds of custody cases. So in the early morning hours of Easter Eve, April 22, 2000, agents of the U.S. Border Patrol's special BORTAC unit, along with more than 130 INS personnel approached the house, knocked on the door, and forced their way inside.

Elian was rescued at gun point from his uncle, and sent back home, to his father in Cuba. We needed more details, but it seemed silly to hold those five guys for *LIFE,* given the outcome of the situation. We had seen a school bus earlier that

had been donated by Rockland County New York, with a sign demanding, "Free the Cuban Five Political Prisoners." (An FYI, The Cuban 5 were released, two were returned to Cuba for health or family reasons, the remaining three as part of the deal for more openness with Cuba in 2015.)

School Bus Donated by Rockland, New York

Chapter 10: Death to Fidel and the Death of Che

Though many seem to wish for more, some suggested getting rid of Fidel, his brother Raul, and their ideology. We began to question how they had retained such tight control. We saw few policia and even fewer soldiers. The answer may be in the constant propaganda we'd seen on billboards and television. Hard to believe that alone, could control the minds of Cubans, many who were quite intelligent. They often expressed solidarity, with the government. Expanding our thinking, we wondered about the effect that our own CIA might have had on Cubans. They have attempted many dirty tricks meant to kill Castro. In return, he flaunted those to Cubans, constantly airing his belief that the USA wanted to take over Cuba!

Inside the Department of Dirty Tricks

"We're not in the Boy Scouts," Richard Helms often said when he ran the CIA. He was correct, of course. Boy Scouts do not ordinarily bribe foreign politicians, invade other countries with secret armies, spread lies, conduct medical experiments, build stocks of poison, pass machine guns to people who plan to turn them on their leaders, or plot to kill men such as Patrice Lumumba, (the first Prime Minister of the Democratic Republic of Congo) Castro, or others who displeased Washington. The CIA did these things, and much more, over a long span of time.

In February 1959, Fidel Castro became the Prime Minister of Cuba. Since then, according to the man who was charged with protecting him for most of his regime, Castro had survived over 600 assassination attempts. Fabian Escalante, the former head of the Cuban Secret Service, claimed that the assassination endeavors break down like this: the Eisenhower administration tried to kill Castro 38 times; Kennedy, 42; Johnson, 72; Nixon, 184; Carter, 64; Reagan, 197; Bush Sr., 16; Clinton, 21. (The accuracy of Escalante's statistics, are in dispute.) There are only so many different ways you can ambush someone, so some of the ways the CIA plotted to kill Castro were pretty wild. Here are just a few of the unorthodox methods considered to oust the Beard.

113

10 Ways the CIA Tried to Kill Castro
Source: The Guardian UK, Stacy Conradt

1. Femme fatale. *Marita Lorenz, just one of many women Castro counted as a mistress, allegedly accepted a deal from the CIA in which she would feed him capsules filled with poison. She managed to get as far as smuggling the pills into his bedroom in her jar of cold cream, but the pills dissolved in the cream. She doubted her ability to force-feed Castro face lotion, and she also just chickened out. According to Lorenz, Castro somehow figured out her plan and offered her his gun. "I can't do it, Fidel," she told him.*
2. Poisoned wetsuit. *While there's nothing suspicious about receiving random diving gear from your enemy right in the middle of the Bay of Pigs Invasion, the CIA gave it a shot. In 1975, the Senate Intelligence Committee claimed it had "concrete evidence"*

of a plan to offer Castro a wetsuit lined with spores and bacteria that would give him a skin disease (and maybe worse). The plan supposedly involved American lawyer James B. Donovan, who would present Castro with the suit when he went to negotiate the release of the Bay of Pigs prisoners. A 1975 Associated Press report said the plan was abandoned "because Donovan gave Castro a different diving suit on his own initiative."

3. Ballpoint hypodermic syringe. *An ordinary-looking pen would be rigged with a hypodermic needle so fine that Castro wouldn't notice when someone bumped into him with the pen and injected him with an extremely potent poison.*

4. Exploding cigar. *But this was no parlor trick – this cigar would have been packed with enough real explosives to take Fidel's head off. In 1967, the Saturday Evening Post reported that a New York City police officer had been propositioned with the idea and hoped to carry it out during Castro's United Nations visit in September 1960.*

5. Contaminated cigar. *They may have given up on the TNT stogie, but the idea of spiking his smokes was still being floated around. The CIA even went as far as to recruit a double agent who would slip Castro a cigar filled with botulin, a toxin that would kill the leader in short order. The double agent was allegedly given the cigars in February of 1961, but he apparently got cold feet.*

6. Exploding conch shell. *Knowing that Castro liked to scuba dive, the CIA made plans to plant an explosive device in a conch shell at his favorite spot. They plotted to make the shell brightly colored and unusual looking so it would be sure to attract Castro's attention, drawing him close enough to kill him when the bomb inside went off.*

7. Nair. *Well, maybe not that brand specifically, but according to that 1975 Senate Intelligence Committee report, the U.S. believed that messing with Castro's beard was messing with the man's power. The CIA figured that the loss of the beard would show Cubans that Castro was weak and fallible. A half-baked scheme was hatched to use thallium salt, the chemical in depilatory products such as Nair, in Castro's shoes or in his cigar. The* *chemical would be absorbed or inhaled and cause the famous facial hair to fall out. (Wait, isn't this like an episode from the old TV show Get Smart?)*

8. LSD. *In what was mostly an effort to discredit Fidel, not kill him, a radio station where Castro was giving a live broadcast would be bombarded with an aerosol spray containing a substance similar to LSD. When Fidel had the requisite freak out live on the air, Cubans would think he had lost his mind and stop trusting him.*

9. Handkerchief teeming with deadly bacteria. *The CIA was seemingly obsessed with covering Fidel in harmful bacteria and toxins, because they also considered giving him a germ-covered hankie that would make him very ill.*

10. Poisoned milkshake. *According to Escalante, the closest the CIA ever came to killing Castro was a deadly dessert drink in 1963. The attempt went awry when the pill stuck to the freezer where the waiter-assassin at the Havana Hilton was supposed to retrieve it. When he tried to un-stick it, the capsule ripped open.*

Imagine how patriotic/nationalistic we citizens of the USA would be if another nation was making attempts like these on the lives of our president, our government, or our citizens. Actually we think it is happening in our country as we write these words. Certain politicians peddle and perpetuate fear and hate toward all Muslims for the terror perpetrated by a few. Quite an effective way to cling to power and control the masses.

The Killing of Che
And the Mystery of his Missing Hands

In Cuba, a legend was born that would transcend even Ernesto Che Guevara's own short-lived dreams. Fidel and his group of misfits defeated Cuban dictator Batista in 1959. Che found the day-to-day work of forming and operating a government to be boring. He soon spread his revolutionary wings, taking the fight for economic equality as far afield as Zaire and the African Congo. Che was a soldier, a warrior, with conviction and purpose. Though his writings and speeches were said to have been eloquent, he was best known for those piercing eyes, long hair, and that beret.

Why Did Che Go to Bolivia?

"Let the world change you and you can change the world"
Ernesto Che Guevara

After having been a part of the Cuban Revolution in 1959 and becoming bored with administration of the country, Che believed that Bolivia was ripe for change. Having witnessed Bolivia's poverty years earlier on his motorcycle, he felt his revolutionary ideology would spread easily throughout the impoverished region. Because of Che's presence in Bolivia, 47 fighters, Cuban, Bolivian, Peruvian, and Argentines joined him. They were fighting Bolivian troops that had been trained in the U.S. and were led by a team of 16 Green Beret. (U.S. Special Forces)

The battles continued until the end of September. In October the Bolivian 2nd Battalion aided by the U.S. military and CIA personnel fought with and captured Che Guevara's small band of rebels. They were taken to Vallegrande, Bolivia, where they spent their final hours. On October 9th, 1967 Ernesto Che Guevara was shot to death by Bolivian soldiers as ordered by CIA operatives.

Ten days after his capture, U.S. ambassador to Bolivia, Douglas Henderson, sent confirmation of Guevara's death to Washington. The evidence included autopsy reports and fingerprint analysis conducted by Argentine police officials on Che's amputated hands. Che's hands were cut off under the supervision of CIA agent Gustavo Villoldo to provide proof that he was actually dead. His body was then secretly buried near a desolate airstrip at Villagrande. The location of his unmarked grave was finally discovered in June, 1997.

The Location of Che's Hands Remains a Mystery

We had cycled north, on Ruta Quarenta, (Route 40) through Argentina and into Bolivia. Though we passed within 100 miles of Villagrande, we didn't try to visit. There are no monuments, only a few reminders and a small chapel memorialize the awful events that took place there in 1967.

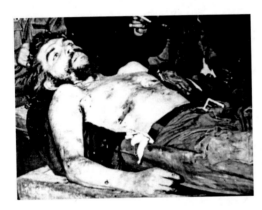

There are varying stories of Che's bravery in the face of the firing squad. After suggesting he was worth more to them alive than dead, he accepted his fate. One account told of a last message to his family. Another told that Che faced them squarely and said, "Look at me as you shoot, you are killing a Man." What a shame such an interesting, obviously charismatic guy, was cut down in his prime at age thirty-nine.

In death, Che remains loathed, by the world's most wealthy capitalists. Not wanting him to appear to have died in battle, the Bolivians, at the direction of the CIA, cleansed his body of the blood, combed his hair, and laid him out in a funeral pose for pictures.

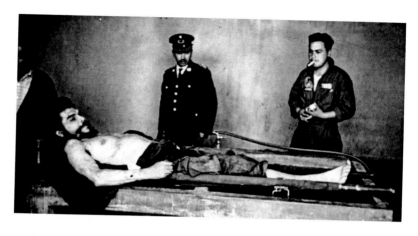

Those Shirts, That Picture

As we cycled through Africa, we'd seen Che on the t-shirts of hundreds of young men. Though he'd been featured on banners and posters proclaiming the values of socialism, his worst nightmare would probably be in finding, that products like Smirnoff Vodka and Taco Bell had used his image to promote their products.

So How Did One So Hated (or Feared) Become an Icon?

Many think Che's fame became iconic, due to Luis Korda's black-and-white photograph of him looking resolute, in his starred beret, his hair flowing, and of course, those piercing eyes. Another famous picture of Che in Cuba, was on a currency note honoring him as Minister of Finance. The powerful Argentinean right-wing military dictatorship of that time, ruled Che was a traitor, to be despised. With the change of government there, he became a national hero. Even an Argentinean postage stamp has been issued honoring Che's Argentinean roots.

Che Guevara is an icon of the 20th Century, both his name and his face are recognized all over the world. Born in Rosario, Argentina in 1928 he was the right-hand of the Cuban Revolution leader, Fidel Castro.

Rosario, Argentina

Unveiling of a statue of Ernesto 'Che' Guevara
China Daily 05/16/2008

Chapter 11: Casa Chela, Old Havana, Havana Luxury?

Walking back to our Casa Particular held a special fascination for me and our camera: the classic cars of Cuba. The crowd back at Casa de Chela was limited to non-English speakers. We lay back under the AC cooling and snoozing. Our in-room TV received only three channels. They cut in and out, often in the middle of a program. One broadcast pretty good English lessons. One was a Cuban soap opera, and the third was the ever popular Fidel Channel. Oh, that guy could ramble.

We didn't get most of his message, but our best guess was that he was telling the story of the Cuban heroes who had fought in Angola. That conflict had been fought by the MPLA (Peoples Movement for the Liberation of Angola) against UNITA (National Union for the Total Independence of Angola) and the National Liberation Front of Angola (FNLA). MPLA was aided by Cuba and the Soviet Union, and UNITA and FNLA were supported by South Africa, the United States, and Zaire. It became Africa's longest running conflict.

Marvin came in as we were eating. He took a seat, smoked one cigarette after another, and begged us to find an American woman who would marry him. We tried to convince him to stop smoking. He was a nice young guy but adjustment to the capitalist lifestyle of the USA might prove to be difficult. He had a pretty good lifestyle there in Cuba. Chela also complained but they both had baubles, trinkets, expensive-looking watches and jewelry. The house was finely furnished and they both spend a lot of time on their cell phones. Yes, Marvin had a cell phone, glued to his ear much of the time. After a long call and cigarette, he resumed his plea for an American woman. I suggested that he had a beautiful girlfriend and wondered why would he want to marry a stranger. He replied, "Oh, American wife would be strictly business." Although, he couldn't explain how he would compensate the American woman.

Makin' the Move

For our final *on the road* breakfast, we ate the last of our cereal wet down with powdered milk. We threw the remaining powdered milk away. It had suspect- looking little black things in it. Man, were we glad that both this chapter of our lives and our Cuban adventure were coming to a close. After a brief goodbye to all family members present, Marvin helped us get the bikes down the stairs. Not that we were tired of our Havana family, we were more than ready to go. Cat was dreaming of Mexican food and a margarita.

We cycled out to the end of the Malecon, then circled back to Wilber's apartment. He was mopping and cleaning. His mother-in-law, Isabela, was working at it, too. Doris, Wilbur's wife, spoke a little English. She introduced us to their new son, Gabriel, then we enjoyed looking at their album of wedding pictures, that had been spared by the flood. It was good seeing Wilber in his family mode and spending time with him away from his workplace. He was definitely a proud father.

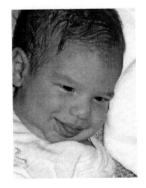

If a Cubana Hocks a Loogie, Turn the Other Cheek

As we prepared to leave, Cat let out a yelp. I thought she'd been bitten by a bug. No, the woman upstairs had leaned over her balcony railing and spit, hocked a loogie, as the kids used to say. Her wad of spittle hit Cat on the cheek. It wasn't intentional, in fact, the woman sent her daughter down to apologize. Ah, just another of our unforgettable Cuban moments.

Wilber pointed out the line on the outside wall, that showed the depth of the flood waters. It had reached six feet deep. We were amazed when he told us, "The government has already replaced our mattresses and a delivered a new TV. Most of our other furniture was okay." The Cuban government seemed to have a good disaster rapid response system. They had even set up a clean drinking water station just across the street and the neighbors were patiently waiting in line.

We prolonged the sweet and sorrow moments then finally hugged, cheek-kissed, and cycled away as they waved. We were hopeful it wouldn't be our final goodbye.

After having walked around the city, we had no problem cycling our way back to the Libre. The bellmen on duty knew nothing of our arrangement to leave the bikes. I followed as the bell captain went to the front desk expressing his disappointment. When I clarified that we were guests of the hotel and would check in the following morning, he conceded. He did condition his approval on our word that we'd take the bikes to our room directly upon checking in. We loved that because we'd feared it would be a fight convincing them to allow our bikes into the room.

A Visit to Habana Vieja

With the afternoon to ourselves, we decided to take a classic caddie taxi to Habana Vieja, Old Havana. The ride and the area, were both a step back in time. Habana Vieja, was almost as quaint and picturesque as Old Cartagena, Colombia. Narrow lanes were lined with old stone buildings. Plazas were full of music and life. It

124

was all about cigars and music. Women and guys dressed in funny clothes posed with tourists for photos with a big cigar. I chose an interesting-looking gal with thick glasses. She was a character, smiling, laughing, and speaking a bit of English. She made it clear that the expensive Cohiba cigar was *NOT* to touch my lips!

We lunched and listened as a group played classic and modern Cuban music. There was a festive feeling in the air. That part of Cuba wasn't mired down in the problems created by super socialism and an ignorant embargo. Plenty of tourists from all over the world danced, drank, and puffed on cigars. We tried to imagine what it would be like if "We, The People" could easily, legally travel and enjoy that wonderful place.

On the way into Havana we'd cycled near the marina where Ernest Hemingway had kept Pilar, his fishing boat. There was a plaque on a hotel memorializing the place where he spent days while writing "The Sun Also Rises." The fisherman character in "The Old Man and The Sea," was said to have been Gregorio, captain of the Pilar. He often posed for pictures. He'd lived and relived his days of glory while picking up a few kooks until recently. He died at age 104.

At Home with Chela and Familia

A taxi back to Chela's and another dinner in. Tonight was spaghetti without sauce. When Cat asked about finding some bread, Marvin asked for fifty cents and walked to the bakery. He returned with a huge bag filled with fresh baked rolls. Once again, we'd gotten to share the socialist advantage. He and friends sat out on the patio smoking. When we finished eating, Marvin turned on some music and they began dancing. Cat and Chela joined in and it was a party. A strange, eclectic sort of family group. Even Assef and his girlfriend seemed to fit in. I asked him when he would go back to Syria. His answer surprised me, "Probably never." His mother and father had moved to London. He felt that he would get a good job there once he has earned his pharmacology degree.

Marvin said, "I have friend, Thomas, he live in San Juan Capistrano, California." When we told him that was very close to our daughter Lori's home, he found Thomas's address and made us promise to send a letter and e-mail, then meet him as we pass through the area on our way home.

PEACE WITHOUT FREEDOM IS TASTELESS
FREEDOM WITHOUT PEACE IS BITTER
WE NEED A BALANCED DIET TO ENJOY LIFE
Pat Patterson, while in Soviet Union, 1989

This idea above about PEACE and FREEDOM was my original thought while visiting the Soviet Union. They did have peace but without many of the freedoms we on the Western side had always taken for granted. On the other side of the coin, freedom at the price of ongoing conflicts is bitter. Since that time, the Russians had loosened up creating new issues and struggles. Afghanistan and Iraq are our USA's example of ongoing, never- ending combat. For Cat and me, the Patriot Act and other actions back home had us wondering where our FREEDOM was going in the ongoing WAR ON TERROR? Our opinion was the USA is stuck in the middle of religious civil wars. Geez, we've unleashed that darned Bicycle Philosopher again. Hey, I says it like I sees it!

As promised, we were allowed to move the bikes to our room as soon as we checked in to Havana Libre. The rest of our day was spent preparing for flight. It took an entire roll of packing tape to cover the rips and holes in our beat-up plaid plastic travel bags.

Cat went out seeking our last taste of Cuban country pizza and found it. Not as cheap or as good as in the little roadside stands, but good. I was up to my elbows in grease getting the bikes ready for travel. I'm getting pretty good at breaking them down and boxing them. We were happy knowing that this should be the last time they would be subjected to this treatment. Yup, no more flying, just the long Mexican bike ride back home to California.

Still too poor to eat out, Cat went down to get a bottle of wine from our nearby favorite little store. Holy Moses, they were closed!

Was it Sunday? Who ever heard of such a thing? Closed on the Sabbath, in this Godless commie country. We were doomed to a couple of beers before dinner. We don't care for beer with food. Sorry beer-drinking friends, it's just not the same as a glass of wine.

Cat pulled supper together by going down to the hotel cafeteria. She ordered, then carried the plates back to our room on her arm. Those college days as a waitress finally paid off. The kitchen crew was duly impressed and applauded as she left, plates on her arm.

Money, Money, Moooonnnneeeey

Cat constantly counted and recounted our diminishing kooks. She feared we'd would go broke and have to stay in Cuba forever. She felt we'd make it with current cash on hand. What we had, she estimated, would pay the excess baggage fee and Cuban departure tax. Perhaps we'd even have a tiny bit left. Yet she still had huge anxiety, she wanted out of Cuba. I asked, "What would they do, throw us in prison?" What would we do? Wilber had said, "There are ways to get U.S. dollars. We send your credit card number to a person in the Florida. He gets cash and sends it via Western Union." The Florida facilitator would charge 20 percent. That sizable fee was for the Cuban who was for taking the risk. Delivery would be in U.S. dollars. Then 20 percent exchange rate loss for kooks. If we wanted $500, we would have to charge $800 on our credit card.

Risk? We would be handing our credit card to a stranger who could take the total allowed credit from the card if they chose to, without any way for us to recover it.

Chapter12: The Great Escape to Cancun

We had to rise early to prepare for the transfer company ride to the Aero Puerto. So anxious to get going, we awoke and were ready two hours early. Anxiety was running high. The huge included breakfast buffet we'd paid for in advance in Cancun, was a delicious send off. It seemed much more abundant and grand, than it had just three weeks earlier.

The van was late, which further spiked our tensions. Once there, the driver fought the rear seats getting them to lay down and make room for the bikes. We tried to help but the driver was like a bull in a Cuban china shop. We figured it was best to stand back and enjoy. That way he couldn't blame us for torn upholstery or chain grease on the seats.

Cubano Air Bagged the Bags and Bikes for FREE!

All that hurry and worry was for naught. Rushing into the airport, we learned there had been a schedule change giving us an extra hour before flight time. So, a three-hour wait. The good news, we were first in the check-in line.

We'd packed the panniers into our plaid plastic bags but left the zippers open, in the event they would want to inspect the contents. The counter clerk assured us it was okay to zip them up. I began taping them tightly to avoid a bag blowout. He came over and asked, "Why you do thees? Cubano Air require all bag be plastic wrap before check in." What a boon for us, they did the wrap for FREE. It was a strange process, different from the Saran wrap process we were accustomed to. They had large plastic bags that slipped over the bikes and bags. Then they used a hot air gun to shrink and seal them. Clever, and a great way to avoid baggage handler theft.

When the counter finally opened, the same guy took us in tow. He ticketed us, then tagged the bags and bikes. He struggled lifting them all onto the scale, then said, "You must pay four CUC for each kilo over weight, but I only charge for ten kilos." That was twenty kilos lighter than we thought it would be, but I couldn't help asking, "Why four CUC, we paid only two CUC on the flight over?" He went across the room, returned and said, "Si, you correcto." He reduced our cost to twenty kooks. What a good man he was.

Next step, the expected departure tax of 25 CUC each. Hey Cubanos, we had money to burn. Well, not enough to do much but we would be able to pay taxi fare in Cancun. I even shopped cigars for a moment or two, thinking it would be fun to send some as gifts to Cat's dad, brother and nephew. The only ones in our price range were generic. The big-name brands like Cohiba were incredibly expensive. A box of the best sold for 522 kooks! Sorry guys, no cigars. Hey they're bad for your health anyway! Cat converted our remaining kooks to Euros.

Aboard the Flying YAK

The Immigration process was strange, indeed. As we started through the doorway of the booth, an officer yelled out indicating each of us had to use separate booths. The officers in the booths did the same intense inspection of our passports, looking at the picture, back at our faces, then back at the pictures. When finished, they stamped the sneaky loose visa page and buzzed the door at the back of the booth open. It was like Alice in Wonderland Through the Looking Glass. We'd both passed the visual inspections and popped out into a waiting area.

When they called our flight for boarding, we lined up and struck up a conversation with Dani, a young guy from Spain. He'd been living in Colorado for five years. When we reached the doorway into the plane, Cat let out a sigh of relief. At the same moment her name came blasting out over a loudspeaker. The uniformed flight attendant pulled us out of line. More anxiety, he took Cat's boarding pass and then had her follow him back to Immigration. Cat's churning stomach relaxed when they explained they'd forgotten to stamp the boarding pass.

On board at last with carry-on bags stowed, they announced there would be a thirty minute delay. Sitting, waiting, the anxiety once again began to build: fueled by fear that we would have to stay in Cuba while they repaired the aging plane or that they'd fly the forty-year-old Russian Yak with a mechanical problem. (*engine problem?*) After an hour and a half the crew began giving us the pre-flight instructions demonstrating seat belts and life vests, then sat down and we all waited. Another announcement: the delay had been extended. We were invited to de-plane and visit the coffee shop. Little good that would do us, we had no Cuban money. Then a good news announcement: Cubano Air would pay for sandwiches and soft drinks.

Standing in line for our "delay sandwich," we again talked with Dani. He said, "I'm an engineer and have been working with a U.S. firm in Colorado. Now, I'm taking time off to explore. I have spent a month in Cuba and I plan on another in Mexico, then head for Central and South America." He got serious and shared an observation, "Most people in the U.S. work much more than Europeans yet generally have no plans to travel. In Europe, most of us work, only to get enough money to travel." We could only agree that most of our fellow countrymen have been conditioned with a fear or hatred for foreign shores.

The announcement to re-board came just as we got to the counter. Hungry, we stood our ground. The deli clerk did away with choices, jammed a sandwich and can of coke into each of our hands, and we dashed back to our seats. Barely time to buckle in and we lifted off. Thank goodness, the flight was smooth as glass.

Reflections on a Place We Learned to LOVE!

Although we were both ready to escape Cuba, we could have used a few more days. The pressure of money and time to catch our pre-ticketed return flight put a bit of a damper on the experience. Life there was definitely different: shades of the old Soviet Union I'd visited in 1989. The two money systems mixed with the infancy of capitalism. Interestingly, a friend in Mexico said, "I believe Cuba is positioned to become a strong economy, like China." The people did generally take great pride in their work, even though the brain surgeon and cane cutter made the same low wages. The universities were world class and affordable. Students come to study from all corners of the world, except the USA, of course.

If you've been to Cuba, we hope you found that we did Cuba and her peoples justice in our stories.
If you haven't been to Cuba, we hope you find them inspiring!

943 Kilometers Cycled in Cuba (almost 600 miles)

A Change by EXECUTIVE ORDER

In 2016, by presidential executive order, many of the restrictions regarding travel and trade with Cuba were lifted. These words spoken by President Obama really made sense to us. *"Decades of U.S. isolation of Cuba have failed to accomplish our objective of empowering Cubans to build an open and democratic country. At times, longstanding U.S. policy towards Cuba has isolated the United States from regional and international partners, constrained our ability to influence outcomes throughout the Western Hemisphere, and impaired the use of the full range of tools available to the United States to promote positive change in Cuba. Though this policy has been rooted in the best of intentions, but has had little effect – today, as in 1961, Cuba is governed by Castro's Communist party.*

We cannot keep doing the same things and expect different results. It does not serve America's interests, or the Cuban people, to try to push Cuba toward collapse. We know from hard-learned experience that it is better to encourage and support reform than

to impose policies that will render a country a failed state. We should not allow U.S. sanctions to add to the burden of Cuban citizens we seek to help."

Fidel is gone, he died in 2016, no intrigue, of natural causes at age 90, no exploding cigars. And, Raul is scheduled to retire in 2018. After fifty nine years will there be a vacuum in leadership. It will be interesting to see how the Cuban Communist Party selects new leadership and how close to the ideals of the REVOLUTION the new leadership will steer the country.

Now President Trump has issued his own presidential executive order reversing many of the advances made under

President Obama. There will definitely be changes in Cuba. As of 2012, there were 1.2 million Cubans in Miami. Trump and the Republican Party see that as a lot of VOTES!

Wish We'd Visited Hemingway's Haunts

Ernest Hemingway owned his Finca Vigia (Lookout Farm) for thirty years. It's just a little less than ten miles east of Havana. T'was there he wrote two of his most famous books, "For Whom the Bell Tolls" and "The Old Man and the Sea." "A Movable Feast"

was written there, as well. After Hemingway's death in 1961, the Cuban government took ownership of the property.

Honestly, we did talk about Hemingway, his home and boat, but we were out of money and time. I most miss that close encounter. He has been an inspiration for us.

What of Castro and Papa Hemingway? It is said that they met only once, at a fishing contest in Hemingway's honor. Castro caught the big one, and won the trophy. Seemingly embarrassed, he said, "I am a novice at fishing." Hemingway replied, "You're a lucky novice."

The Ambos Hotel gained international note due to its most famous long-time tenant: in 1932 a room on the upper (5th) floor became the "first home" in Cuba for writer Ernest Hemingway, who enjoyed the views of Old Havana, and the harbor sea in which he fished frequently in his yacht *Pilar*. Hemingway rented the room for $1.50 per night ($1.75 for double occupancy) until mid-1939. Hemingway began his novel "For Whom the Bell Tolls," a novel of the Spanish Civil War, in that room in the Ambos Mundos, on March 1, 1939.

When we return, this hotel and the bar, El Florida, where Hemingway held court over drinks, will be on our bucket list.

Where Do Pat & Cat Fit In the POLITICAL SCHEME?

Communists? NO! Although we have been called commies and socialists. Pat & Cat's families were both Republican. If you mean extreme Socialists in countries like Cuba and Venezuela, NO. However, if you mean the humanistic, brotherhood type of socialism found in all of the Scandinavian counties, then, YES! Their style of socialism has for years created a very harmonious society. After four straight years of being voted "The happiest country in the world," Denmark just came in second to Norway. What can we of the USA learn from this? We have advanced to fourteenth place but with the current political climate generating fear and hate, it remains to be seen whether we can hold position! We love to be HAPPY, don't you?

As we traveled, our feelings have drawn us into the middle ground. (*Upon return home we registered as Independents.*)

Fidel Castro Meets with Popes

Fidel Castro met with Pope John Paul II in 1998. Pope Benedict traveled to Cuba and met with Castro in 2012. In 2015, Pope Francis met with Fidel. Though Fidel claimed to be an atheist, it seems to us it is possible that as death neared, with his early Catholic upbringing, he may have been more aptly described as agnostic.

Fidel on Religion

According to the Washington Post, former President of Cuba Fidel Castro's letters from prison in 1955 suggest that he "was a man of unusual spiritual depth – and a fervent believer in God." Writing to the father of a fallen comrade, Castro writes: *I will not speak of him as if he were absent, he has not been and he will never be. These are not mere words of consolation. Only those of us who feel it truly and permanently in the depths of our souls can comprehend this. Physical life is ephemeral, it passes inexorably. . .*

This truth should be taught to every human being – that the immortal values of the spirit are above physical life. What sense does life have without these values? What then is it to live? Those who understand this and generously sacrifice their physical life for the sake of good and justice – how can they die? God is the supreme idea of goodness and justice.

Castro was baptized and raised a Roman Catholic as a child but did not practice as one. Pope John XXIII excommunicated Castro in 1962, after he suppressed Catholic institutions in Cuba. Castro has publicly criticized what he sees as elements of the Bible that have been used to justify the oppression of both women and people of African descent throughout history.

In 1992, Castro agreed to loosen restrictions on religion and even permitted church-going Catholics to join the Communist Party of Cuba. He began describing his country as "secular" rather than "atheist". Christmas was banned as a public holiday in 1969. During Pope John Paul's visit he urged Fidel Castro to reinstate Christmas as a public holiday. A year later it was approved and became an official law.

The Cars That Made Cuba Famous

It seems fitting to highlight this story with the some of the remaining photos we have of the 1950s American made cars that have made Cuba famous around the world. Yes, they show plenty of wear and tear but the constant care and ingenuity of the Cuban's have kept them on the road for almost 60 years. There are no new auto parts stores on the island. Yes, they may be held together with bubble gum and bailing wire but to us they were Cuban ART!

McKeel Hagerty, an insurance agent specializing in collector cars said, "When I went to Havana, I jumped in a 1956 Cadillac and it looked really good. The guy turned the key and I heard a Peugeot diesel engine." He likened Cuba to a "Galapagos Island" of cars. "Cuba has been cut off for so long, the cars have morphed into their own species. It's wasn't a Cadillac. It was something else."

Transportation, they call her "The Camel"

The "Camel" above, and the four vehicles on page 141, were manufactured in Russia, or other East Bloc nations. Most of the American classics, as Mr. Hagerty had said, are powered by Russian or other obtainable engines.

Why Did We Decide to Cycle Cuba?
*Was It Because They Cut Off His F***'n Hands?*

It has been verified by those present at the execution of Che, that his hands were cut off and fingerprinted. Also, an impression of Che's teeth was taken. His hands were sent to La Paz, the Bolivian capital then on to Buenos Aires, Argentina for fingerprint matching. They mysteriously disappeared there. Some say they saw them in a jar of formaldehyde. The only thing known for sure, they exist and one day an aspiring capitalist will sell them for millions!

Sorry Che!